WINTER GARDENING

IN THE
MARITIME NORTHWEST

WINTER GARDENING

IN THE
MARITIME NORTHWEST

COOL SEASON CROPS FOR
THE YEAR-ROUND GARDENER

BINDA COLEBROOK

Sasquatch Books
Seattle

First edition published in 1977 by the Tilth Association
Second edition published in 1984 by Maritime Publications

Library of Congress Cataloging-in-Publication Data

Colebrook, Binda
  Winter gardening in the maritime Northwest.

  Includes index.
  1. Vegetable gardening—Northwest, Pacific. I. Title. II. Title: Cool season crops for the year-round gardener.
SB321.C66   1989   635.09795   89-6046
ISBN 0-912365-21-8

Design by Fran Porter Milner
Typeset in Century
Production by Weekly Typography & Graphic Design, Seattle

  Peter Warshall: page 3, reprinted with permission from *Shelter*, 1973, Shelter Publications, Bolinas, California.
  Jody Aliesan: "Waiting," page 25, reprinted with permission from *Soul Claiming*, 1974, Mulch Press, Northampton, Massachusetts.
  Shunryu Suzuki: pages 32 and 64, reprinted with permission from *Zen Mind, Beginner's Mind*, 1970, John Weatherhill, Inc., New York, New York.
  David A. Stone: page 28, reprinted with permission from *Know and Grow Vegetables 2*, by P. J. Salter and J. K. A. Bleasdale, 1982, Oxford University Press, Oxford, England.
  M. Nieuwhof: page 74, reprinted with permission from *Cole Crops*, 1969, CRC Press, Inc., Boca Raton, Florida.
  David Mackenzie: pages 119–120, reprinted with permission from *Goat Husbandry*, 1956, Faber and Faber, London, England.

Illustrations:
  Robert Willamson: "Leek Unfolding," pages 18–19, reprinted with permission from Abundant Life Seed Foundation; 20, 30, 55–56, 65, 74, 76, 79, 81, 83, 87, 88, 89, 91, 93, 96, 98, 99, 103, 106, 110, 111, 114, 124.
  Carol Oberton: pages 1, 4, 5, 6, 7, 36, 37, 47, 48, 59, 92, 120.
  Rebecca Samson: dedication page and pages 8, 36, 39, 40, 73, 80.
  Gerrit Byeman & Associates: pages 57, 62.
  Bob Benson: map on page 4.

Sasquatch Books
1931 Second Avenue
Seattle, Washington 98101
(206) 441-5555

Other gardening titles from Sasquatch Books
  Growing Vegetables West of the Cascades
  The Year in Bloom
  Three Years in Bloom

CONTENTS

PREFACE

In the time before and during World War II, most serious gardeners in the maritime Northwest knew that selected vegetable varieties could be overwintered to enliven many a winter meal. Several seed companies and at least one book (*Growing Vegetables in the Pacific Northwest* by Cecil Solly) promoted those varieties and the techniques for successful winter gardening.

By the sixties, though, much of this knowledge was being ignored or had been forgotten except by a faithful few. Fresh produce from California was plentiful and cheap, and most people were too busy enjoying the post-war boom to garden. Many of middle age associated vegetable gardening with the poverty of the Depression and the scarcities of wartime.

But I was part of a younger group of people who again hungered for more contact with the earth. So, when I arrived in Seattle in the spring of 1971, as soon as I had found shelter with friends I sought out the next most important thing to me—a spot in which to grow a garden. In fact, I found two spots: one in the then-new P-Patch at 25th NE and NE 80th, and one behind the house I moved into on Capitol Hill. Both gardens were already growing plants, so I had the pleasure of just weeding and tending them, without any of the anxieties of having to find out what grew well in this radically different part of the world (I'd come from the East Coast via Wisconsin).

I went traveling that fall; when I came back in December, the Capitol

Hill garden was weedy and devoid of veggies. But the P-Patch, much to my surprise, had great lovely plants of kale and parsley scattered through it. With delight, I dug a few of both and took them home in a cardboard box. Before I had time to plant them again, though, it started to snow.

It was an outstanding blizzard by Seattle standards; the snow stayed on the ground for several weeks. When it melted, there were the plants, sitting happily in their dark, safe container, fresh as the day I had lifted them.

That was my introduction to the strange, wonderful, mild winters of the Pacific Northwest. Seeing that the ground had never frozen, I dug some holes (and in the process discovered a few of the summer's carrots, as sweet and crisp as in July) and put in the kale and parsley. We ate them till May.

In October I moved to another house, in Leschi by Lake Washington, with an even better winter-garden site. It was a little late for starting plants. Nonetheless, I went down to the Seattle Garden Center to talk to Bob Gill (whose family had run Gill Brothers Seeds) and discovered a dedicated group of people there who made the effort to grow fresh vegetables all winter.

Bob sold me some onion sets, garlic, and raab, gave me as much advice as he could, and I was on my way. The bulbs did well, but the raab was stunted by the wet, infertile soil I had chosen for it. I didn't yet have a firm grasp of the underlying principles of winter cropping; those became clearer after a year or so. By the winter of 1974–75, I was able to produce all of my own winter vegetables on only 720 square feet of moderately sunny ground.

In the spring of 1975, Rick Erickson, then the produce manager of Puget Consumers' Co-op, convinced me that I should find out what other gardeners were doing year-round, teach some classes, and see if it was commercially feasible for farmers to produce winter vegetables for the co-op. Thanks to Rick's and the co-op's commitment to having fresh local produce available, the PCC initiated the Winter Garden Project.

By the fall of that year, there were 15 participants in the project, sharing ideas, successes, and failures with me. Some were in Seattle, the rest divided among Whidbey, Lopez, Orcas, and Port Townsend. We got some maximum/minimum thermometers to see at what point different varieties would freeze out, and I went around visiting the participants' gardens, observing what did and didn't happen.

I wouldn't want you to get the idea that this was anything fancy or that it could be called "scientific" research. We were just a group of gardeners encouraging each other to be less dependent on trucked-in vegetables, figuring out when different varieties had to be sown, and enjoying the excitement of homegrown lettuce in January.

Around this time, I also joined Tilth, a group of rural and urban people who supported regional agriculture. In the following spring, I moved again—this time out of the city, to Pragtree Farm near Arlington, Washington. I spent a year and a half there working with Tilth members who were growing vegetables on a commercial scale. This was very different from small-scale gardening. The farm is in the foothills of the Cascades, so the climate is much colder than in the Puget Sound Basin. This enabled me to test the hardiness of many varieties—and to begin to understand what commercial farmers are up against.

While at the farm, I began to locate new cold-hardy varieties. Some of these were Asian, but most were from England and Europe. I also started to seek out comprehensive gardening books and seed catalogs from the British Isles. Had I spoken other languages and had better contacts, I would have investigated Japanese, Danish, Dutch, Belgian, and French sources, as well. In any case, the few books that I did get my hands on convinced me that the art of winter gardening was still alive in Britain and Europe.

In 1977, I wrote the first edition of *Winter Gardening* with encouragement from Mark Musick, then president of Tilth. Tilth published it, funded by a loan from the Corner Green Grocery Collective and a loan and grant from Puget Consumers' Co-op.

Now, 12 years later, I am happy and delighted that the book has been so useful for so long to so many gardeners, farmers, and other horticulturists. My thanks to all who have helped me to make this a better, more accurate, and up-to-date edition. I am especially grateful to those who have been inspired by the ideas presented here and taken them several steps further. Their efforts benefit local gardening and farming, and thus provide the people of this region with healthier and more enjoyable food.

Happy gardening, and *bon appétit*!

February 1989
Alm Hill
Nooksack, Washington

For the mist people, for the fish people,
for the wave and the rock and the fern people.
For the madrone, and the cloud,
  and the wind people,
the gull and the crow and the grass people.

For the clod and the worm,
the slug and the duck,
for all of the beetle and fly people.

For the sheep and the goat,
the cabbage and the rose,
for the mouse people,
and also the house people.

All my relations, all my relations.

WHAT THIS
BOOK IS ABOUT

I wrote this book for people living in the maritime Northwest who would like to have more fresh vegetables in their gardens during the winter months. It will be especially useful to those who, having learned their gardening in a continental climate, are not aware of the possibilities of a maritime climate and hence close up their gardens from October till May. Even people who have grown up here and gardened in this mild environment may appreciate a reminder of the many winter varieties and good seed sources available to them.

This book is about vegetable and herb varieties that regularly come a crop between October and May. These are often termed cool-season or cool-weather crops. They are not *sown* in the winter, but *harvested* then. While some sowings can be made as early as February and March or as late as October, most are done from April through September.

If you think about this for a bit, you will see that growing winter crops means that you turn from a summer gardener into a *year-round gardener* (a lot more work, by the way!). I suppose I really should have written a book about year-round gardening, but if I had done that, I would have had to devote space to tomatoes and cucumbers, when it is the cool-season crops that need to be discussed. Also, you might have missed the point: in this climate, you don't have to be without vegetables in the fall, winter, and early spring if you use suitable varieties, observe the right sowing dates, understand the principles of cool-season production, and experiment for yourself!

WHAT THIS BOOK IS ABOUT

THE PRINCIPLES OF
WINTER GARDENING

Climate

mama earth

The earth turns eastward round her poles. Our main wind comes to us from the west, across hours of ocean, damp and restless. That mass of ocean air gives us our climate, known as maritime, from the coast to the Cascade Mountains. This climate is just what is needed for winter gardens in the higher latitudes. It exists naturally along *west* coasts, peninsulas, and islands from about 37 to 59 degrees latitude, give or take a bit due to ocean currents and other factors. If you look at a world map, you will see that parts of Europe, Japan, Tasmania, the south island of New Zealand, and Chile are all within this range. In North America, the area from northern California to northern Vancouver Island in British Columbia and parts of the Alexander Archipelago are also suitable. Farther north, although the coastal climate is mild, there is little arable land, and high precipitation and lack of winter daylight prevent most winter crop production.

A maritime climate is distinguished by its cool, even, humid nature, both summer and winter. Here on the west coast of North America, temperatures hover around 40°F in the winter, with occasional changes in either direction. Spring and fall are long, slow affairs—misty, cloudy, and rainy—trying to the patience of the human inhabitants.

For vegetables, however, this murky weather is easier to deal with than the sharp, dry cold and sudden temperature changes of a continental climate. In fact, *many* of our common vegetables are well adapted to it. The long falls that gradually turn colder give vegetables ample time to prepare for winter and *harden up*. When the first frosts come, they are usually accompanied by high soil moisture and high air humidity. The latent heat in this water vapor is returned to the air as the water condenses in the form of frost, preventing sudden drops in temperatures. Misty mornings are another plus, as they give frozen plants plenty of time to thaw out gradually before they are touched by the sun. (Later, in the long, cool springs, plants can produce lots of growth before bolting with warm weather and longer days.)

Winter does come, though! Around the time of the winter solstice, the dry, cold air masses east of the sheltering mountains tend to flow over and bring a week or two of continental-type weather to us. Snow, though hard on traffic, is a blessing to the garden as it protects the soil and plants from freezing, insulating them in a snug white blanket. It is when cold comes *without* precipitation, the soil freezes deeply for long periods of time, and dry winds blow that you can expect to lose many of your winter vegetables.

The winter of 1978–79 was like that in Washington, with frigid weather from Thanksgiving until February. But still, in my garden in Whatcom County near the Canadian border, leeks, kale, parsnips, and mulched carrots supplied winter food. And in March the unprotected spinach and corn salad, along with the lettuces under the cold frames, all revived, grew, and produced an abundance of salads. Sometimes these cold years run in bunches, as they did in the 1950s. It's hard to tell when they will come, but you can count on at least one year in five not being very good for winter crops. Every 25 years or so, the maritime Northwest gets a really rough winter like 1978–79. But even these aren't as bad as an average continental winter.

Different parts of the Northwest have variations on the general maritime theme. The whole coastal strip is milder and very rainy and windy. All the foothills are colder in winter, with shorter and often cooler growing seasons. The inland valleys of southern Washington and the Willamette Valley in Oregon have slightly warmer summers and colder winters, while the Puget Sound region is generally mild. The San Juan Islands experience less rain but more wind and cooler summers. Wherever you live, in order to be successful with winter crops you must pay attention to your local climate. By experimenting you can discover which winter varieties are suited to your garden and the proper time to sow and transplant them.

Knowing that nothing, not even the Earth you are standing on, is standing still, is part of the Earth-shelter-yoga. The more you feel these vibrations (the whole biosphere breathing as a lung and exchanging energy like the breath), the greater joy this more accurate and truthful Energy Earth will bring.

So find happiness in the fog, in mud, and dust. This is a plea not to indulge in criticism of the weather. As seashores sluff away and deserts turn to meadows, we are being entertained by the three states of matter that were the conditions for our life.

—Peter Warshall

Site

The best site for fall and winter crops is a gentle slope on the south side of a hill or a building. It might be a site you could terrace, with wind protection close enough to make a difference but not so close it blocks the sun. A building reflects and holds heat; the slope aids in drainage; terraces make a warm microclimate; and wind protection allows that pocket of warm air to stay where it has developed.

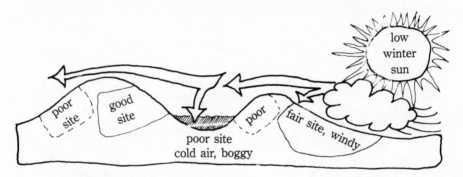

Light and warmth

Usually the best place for winter crops is also a good sunbathing spot, so let that be your guide. When the sun comes out for a week during one of those January–February high-pressure systems, you should be able to work comfortably in your shirtsleeves in the perfect site. (I did in my Seattle garden, even though just around the north corner of the garage it was still winter.) That extra warmth means extra growth on your lettuce, corn salad, Brussels sprouts, etc., and therefore healthier plants and more food. It also means warmer temperatures at night, which can make the difference between losing your plants to freezes or not.

Many a less-than-ideal spot, however, has produced an abundance of winter vegetables. If your choices for a garden don't include a particularly sunny spot (at least half a day of sun in the summer), then you may have to limit the kinds of vegetables you will grow. Better to have lots of spinach, lettuce, and corn salad than Brussels sprouts and cabbages that won't make it (especially if you are more likely to eat the former raw and hence maximize your nutrition).

I have always underestimated the effects of shade and soil type on timing and size of plants. Then for two years I gardened in two different sites at the same time. One was on a northeast-facing slope with a light silt soil, and it didn't get sun until around 10 in the morning. The other, two miles away, was down on river-bottom land and received a full day of sun. I took starts from the same plug flat and planted some out at each site on the same day. Two weeks later, I could see the difference: by the end of the month, the lowland plants were twice the size of the hillside ones. If I had been gardening only at the hillside site, I would have thought I was losing my touch!

If your only sunny spot faces onto a busy street, beware: traffic exhaust will be coating your plants, soil, and, what's worse, your lungs with lead, asbestos, and other nasties. My best advice is to move, but if you can't, be sure to wash your food well and avoid the garden during rush hour.

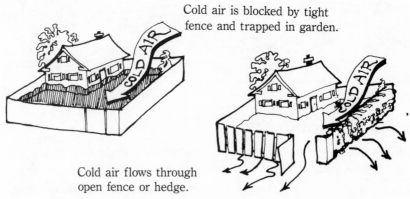

Cold air is blocked by tight fence and trapped in garden.

Cold air flows through open fence or hedge.

The warmest spot in fall and winter is usually the south side of a house, a traditional site of the perennial flower beds. If you like flowers, that's a hard thing to give up. Consider interplanting with some of the more striking winter vegetables. Kales are both beautiful and delicious, and lettuce or onion greens can be tucked in among the asters. Be careful, though: many garden flowers and bulbs are poisonous, and you wouldn't want to eat a daffodil bulb thinking it was an onion.

Keep in mind that soil near house walls often contains chips and flakes of paint. If you live in an older house, chances are that the paints used were lead-based. Some municipalities will test for lead. If you're unsure, the safest thing to do is to remove the suspect soil and replace it.

Drainage

Drainage of both water and air is another very important aspect of a site. Low spots are poor choices for winter gardens, because they collect cold air as well as water. Wet soil will be too cold for good growth and it will suffocate your plants, which need air around their roots. Too much moisture can also increase problems with rot. If there are water drainage problems in the middle of an otherwise desirable spot, it is worth the trouble to install tile, dig a diverting ditch, or make raised beds.

You can also have air drainage problems in the middle of a slope if you have barriers to the free flow of air. A tight fence *downhill* of your garden will catch the freezing air instead of letting it pass on by. Use an open fence or hedge instead. However, a solid barrier *uphill* is all to the good, as it deflects cold air and drying winds from the garden.

Shelter

No matter how good your site is in other respects, if the wind can blow away the warm air that has been built up, it won't do the plants much good. Plants are quite vulnerable to wind damage in the winter. For one thing, they become brittle and desiccated in freezing weather; for another, if the ground is soft from lots of rain, their roots can easily be dislodged.

There are two distances at which windbreaks are useful: relatively long distances of 50 feet or more (provided by tall structures such as houses, barns, or trees); and distances less than 40 feet (provided by garden fences, hedges, and shingles or cloches). Unless you're using transparent cloches, you should make sure that your wind protection doesn't block the low winter sun.

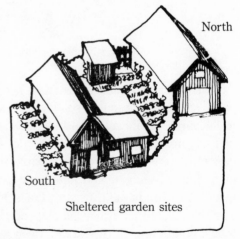

Sheltered garden sites

Given enough space, I think it's worthwhile to make a walled garden out of whatever material you can round up. If you can control the design of your house and outbuildings, take a tip from the layout of European and New England farms, which are often built in a complex that leaves sheltered spaces. In the New England countryside the houses and barns used to be connected, but that is a fire hazard and probably should be avoided. Hedges or fences connecting buildings would serve just as well. In the city or suburbs this protection occurs automatically from the small size of lots and the proximity of buildings.

If you want to make a windbreak for your garden or grounds you have to decide what form to use. Although fences are expensive, they are quick to build and are good if you have limited space. A hedge may take five years to reach a useful size, and you have to keep it pruned well at first to encourage density. It also occupies a lot of space.

A solid barrier yields a sheltered area 8 times the height of the barrier but increases turbulence.

A 40 percent permeable barrier yields a sheltered area 16 times the height of the barrier.

Whichever you choose, fence or hedge, a 40 percent permeability is preferred. This is because solid barriers provide a shorter range of shelter to leeward and increase turbulence. So consider using a slatted fence or hedging material that isn't too dense. Deciduous shrubs tend to be dense in summer and *too* permeable in the winter (with the exception of hedging beech, which keeps its leaves until spring), so one of the evergreens might be a better choice for your main planting. With the wealth of plant material available, you can choose varieties that will grow to the height and thickness you desire. You can also consider including plants that are edible or medicinal, either for you or your livestock. For more on hedges, see Appendix B, Winter Crops for Livestock, and Appendix D, Further Reading.

Soil

A great deal can be said about the nature of soil in relation to vegetable gardening. For the purposes of this book, I will restrict myself to what is relevant to cold-hardy crops. If you want more general information, check the titles in Appendix D. Several of these books have excellent discussions of the nature of soil and its improvement or maintenance in the garden.

To begin with, if you want decent winter crops, you must follow the same procedures of good soil care that you would use to produce decent summer crops—only more so! This is because winter is a time of greater stress for most plants. Also, soil that is to overwinter crops must be well drained. You can't expect much from your kale or spring cabbage, and especially your parsnips, if they have been standing in soggy ground for a month.

Soil *type* also affects cool-season crops considerably. Light soils with plenty of sand warm up quickly and drain well. They are good for later winter sowings and early spring crops. However, because they are not very moisture retentive and are rapidly influenced by temperature changes, light soils do not grow as fine nor as hardy a fall or midwinter crop. This is especially true for members of the brassica family, which are in the main such heavy feeders. A silt or clay loam, on the other hand, will be more complicated to improve, trickier to work, and slower to warm; however, because such a soil can hold more moisture and nutrients, it can grow excellent late crops.

The chances are that you don't have much choice about your garden's soil type and will have to make do with amending it to improve its suitability. Probably the single most important thing you can do as a year-round gardener is to add organic matter, especially in the form of compost and green manure residues. An extension agent I spoke to some years back recommended increasing organic matter content by up to 40 percent of the *worked* volume of the soil. This increases the *humus* content, which aids in balancing the soil's pH and makes the whole gardening process easier and more fruitful. In terms of cool-season production, humus has several roles. It aids in aeration, acts as a buffer of pH, and allows a slower but longer-lasting release of nutrients. During the cold seasons the presence of humus aids in holding a more even soil temperature so that plant roots do not suffer such extremes. For more on humus's biochemical properties, read page 274 of Wolf Storl's *Culture and Horticulture* (see Appendix D).

Some of the best means for adding humus to your soil are green manuring, fallowing, adding animal manure or vegetable composts, and mulching.

There are many different methods of making compost, and, as almost every organic gardening book will tell you how, I am spared that task. Composting is an important practice, and no doubt you will work out a method that suits you.

Green manures

Green manuring is a very useful, if not essential, component of soil care for year-round gardening in a maritime climate, and you would do well to include it in your gardening routine. Our high rainfall and frequent cloud cover guarantee a leached soil, which means an acid soil. Minerals and other nutrients are carried down into the subsoil by the steady rain. These nutrients can be kept in the topsoil by root activity, which also enhances soil life and helps control erosion. Overwintering vegetables and green manures both do this. Green manures are crops that are grown in parts of the garden or fields for a period of time and are worked directly into the soil just before the space is needed. Green manuring is a very ancient practice, used in China for at least 3,000 years and in the Mediterranean for 2,000. It was not employed in northern Europe until the seventeenth century (a fallowing system was used instead). Each region grew many different plants for the process, according to availability and season.

A green manure can grow in the soil for as long as a year (at which point it is really a form of fallowing, but the purpose and end result are similar). In our area, green manures are used most often on a more temporary basis, if they are used at all. It is sometimes difficult to find seed for green manures. Check with Abundant Life, Chase Compost Seeds, Johnny's Selected Seeds, and Territorial Seed Company, which have offered green manure seed in their catalogs (see Appendix C), or try your local feed and seed store.

Suitable green manures include grasses such as rye, winter wheat, and oats, mustards, herbs, and legumes. Rye (*Secale cereale*) is typically used by farmers in this area for a winter cover crop; it is readily available and cheap. Its one great advantage is its ability to germinate and grow in low temperatures. You can sow rye after your late harvests. Unfortunately, rye is so vigorous that it is hard to kill in the spring. In a wet year, when you cannot work your ground enough to kill the rye, it often ends up intercropped with your spinach and peas. Oats (*Avena sativa*) and winter wheat (*Triticum aestivum*) are alternatives to rye. In northern areas some varieties of oats winter-kill, but they continue to hold the soil. Winter wheat will survive even extreme cold. Though oats must be sown early in the fall, they are good for beds intended for the earliest spring sowings. Common vetch or tares (*Vicia sativa*), California bluebell (*Phacelia campanularia*), radish, buckwheat, and pod peas are also good late catch crops that will usually winter-kill in the North.

If you have trouble finding organic forms of nitrogen or can't afford to buy them, legumes, in a mix or alone, are a preferred green manure. Fava beans, winter vetch (*Vicia villosa*), hairy vetch (*Vicia hirsuta*), wild lupines, Austrian field peas (*Pisum arvense*), and crimson clover (*Trifolium incarnatum*) are good ones. Except for the lupines, they are all easier to remove in the early spring than rye, and they leave varying amounts of nitrogen, as well as root residues, in the soil. (These roots play an important part in making the soil friable and suitable for the next crops.)

Green manures also suppress the growth of winter weeds. They can be undersown in vegetables in the later summer or early fall. Some good combinations are: crimson clover or common vetch among leeks, kales, and cabbages; fava beans between the perennial onions; late sowings of vetch with spinach or chicory. The main idea is not to overwhelm your vegetable crop, so choose a green manure with a suitable growth habit or sowing time.

Another important use for green manures is on empty beds that are waiting for summer-sown winter crops. If you have such a bed open for more than three weeks at midsummer, it will substantially aid the following crop to sow it to buckwheat (*Fagopyrum esculentum*). A bed that is open for a little longer can have a clover added in. This will discourage weeds, keep the soil from drying out, and add some organic matter and nitrogen when the green manure is worked or tilled in before transplanting. Remember to work in the green manure a good week before sowing or transplanting the new crop. The initial breakdown products are not good for young plants.

Fallowing

If your garden is large enough, and especially if you have problems with a hard pan, a heavy clay soil, or an excessively light, sandy one, fallowing is a good practice. This consists of taking part of your garden—one-seventh is traditional—and sowing it to green manure crops for the full year. Deep-rooting biennials such as chicory, or legumes such as sweet clover (*Melilotus* spp.), Persian clover (*Trifolium resupinatum*), and alfalfa (*Medicago sativa*), are particularly useful. Buckwheat and California bluebell (sometimes called Bee's Friend) are good annuals to put in the mix to bloom the first year. Rye grass is good for bulk in the topsoil. To avoid competition with vigorous summer weeds, early spring or late-summer sowings may be best; you can adjust these sowing times to suit your site and garden schedule.

Fallowed sections or beds should be mowed occasionally and the cuttings either composted or left to decompose on the soil. This way minerals that are brought up from the subsoil by the roots of the plants are available in the topsoil for the vegetable you grow the following year. The roots also open up passages in the subsoil, helping to aerate it, and add organic matter as they decay.

Fallowing, like green manuring, makes use of the fact that different species of plants utilize and concentrate different nutrients, grow at different rates, have different diseases and pests, and respond to different seasons in their growth patterns. For the price of the seed (or less, if you save your own), you can have a host of green friends working for you in your garden. This makes your garden somewhat more like a natural ecosystem. You are encouraging biological processes and de-emphasizing industrial and mechanical ones.

Mulches

Where you have not had a chance to grow a green manure, a simple hay mulch will at least protect the soil and leave it in a better condition for spring sowing. Mulching is an excellent way to increase organic matter if it's used with discretion. I try to mulch those overwintering crops that stay in the open till April or May. This helps protect their roots and stems during freezing weather and encourages biological activity in the surface soil. It also suppresses weeds from late February through April, a period of active weed growth. True, mulch harbors slugs, but with the bigger winter plants I don't find the damage to be as much of a problem as weedy spots in the spring.

Clearly you want to choose your mulches to suit each crop. For instance, leeks need a finer mulch than kale or cabbages (or even better, a green manure). I don't mulch any spring or early summer sowings; in the wet, cool maritime climate, the soil needs to warm up and lose some moisture. (This is less true of sandy soils than of silt and clay.) Nor do I mulch in frames or under low crops such as corn salad that cover the ground well by the end of October.

Soil *color* also affects crops grown in the cool seasons. The darker a soil is, the better it absorbs heat. This heat is then radiated back out at night, ameliorating temperature swings. For this reason, English gardeners used soot from their stoves as a fine mulch around early crops. Adding organic matter also darkens the soil—yet another reason for using it.

Fertilization

Correct fertilization procedures are good for any garden, but a proper balance of the major nutrients—nitrogen, phosphorus, and potassium (N, P, and K)—is particularly important to cold-season crops. Gardeners tend to concern themselves most with nitrogen, but phosphorus and potassium materially aid in bringing a plant to maturity and hardening it for the winter, so these three must be in balance without an excess of nitrogen. You'll often hear such gardening advice as, "Well, Swiss chard and spinach are leafy greens, and therefore you should give them high nitrogen fertilizers to stimulate leaf production." Ignore this—the fast, sappy growth produced by such nitrogen is just what you *don't* want for hardy fall crops. The first deep frost will do them in. Though you might not get quite as much *fall* production out of a plant that is grown with balanced nitrogen, you will get more winter and early spring production because your plants will *survive* the winter. When the weather begins to warm up in late February or early March, then you can think of side-dressing with a nitrogenous material or foliar-feeding with fish emulsion or the like to produce a flush of growth. If you need it, that is. Some soils, especially certain loams and clays, need spring boosting infrequently, if at all.

One soil I gardened on in the past was not particularly high in nitrogen, but the overwintering spinach and lettuce put on as much growth as I could keep up with in the spring. In general, fall-sown spinach and other winter annuals bolt much later than spring-sown crops. I suspect that this is because they have had all winter to develop a marvelous root system that early spring-sown crops cannot equal. I find the fall spinach tastes better, too: it has a meaty, dark green, sweet quality that I don't find in the spring-sown ones.

Lists of materials high in the macronutrients can be found in Rodale's *Encyclopedia of Organic Gardening.* Many green-manure crops are good phosphorus accumulators: lupines, sweet clover, buckwheat, turnips, and mustards. If you feel you need a better understanding of the role of NPK in plant nutrition, read the relevant sections in Jerry Belanger's *Soil Fer-*

tility (see Appendix D).

Other elements may also help plants develop hardiness: calcium and silicon, for example, and perhaps some of the micronutrients and growth hormones in seaweed. The literature I have read on the subject is controversial. Check some of the books in Appendix D to find out more on this subject.

Another traditional way to add organic matter to your garden is by using animal manures. These are best composted before going on the garden and should include only limited amounts of dry, carbonaceous materials such as hay, straw, or wood products (wood shavings or sawdust). Hay and straw are more typically used in the continental climates and Europe. Most gardening and farming books are written for these areas and assume that animals are bedded in these materials. Such barn cleanings compost quickly and completely in four to six months, or at most a year. However, on the West Coast, most farmers use the more readily available wood products to bed their animals. Sawdust shavings are high in carbon and various lignins and generally need three to four times as much nitrogen and time to decompose as hay and straw do.

Often the percentage of sawdust to manure in barn cleanings is such that the nitrogen in the manure is used up in the process of partially decomposing the sawdust. If the cleanings have sat around in the rain for a while, it's likely that much of the nitrogen will have been leached out. When this mixture is put on the garden, the decomposing bacteria will draw nitrogen from the soil to finish the job. According to Darrell Turner, a retired agronomist formerly with the Washington State University Research Station at Puyallup, this process may tie up the nitrogen for as long as a year.

This doesn't mean that you should avoid manure mixed with wood products, only that you should make an effort to add supplemental nitrogen and allow more time for composting. It is hard to suggest just how much nitrogen you should add. Most sources recommend adding 3½ pounds of actual nitrogen per cubic yard of *raw* sawdust. With barn cleanings you should need less. But really, the only way to tell is to watch the action of the compost pile. If it does not heat up and the wood particles do not break down, you will need to add nitrogen. If, after the pile has cooled off and the worms begin to enter, you still find *lots* of wood particles, you may be able to finish the process by adding more nitrogenous materials. If you still find a few particles at the end of a year, don't worry. At that point they will break down very slowly and will not tie up much nitrogen. These particles will also serve to aerate and loosen the soil, which is helpful if you are working with clay or compacted silts.

If you are bedding your own animals and can control the process, well and good. Straw is the preferred bedding. If this is unavailable or expensive, *hardwood* sawdust is the next best. Alder, maple, and birch are common local trees, and you might find hardwood sawdust from oak or other imported woods at a furniture manufacturer. If you get your sawdust from a local mill, choose a time when they are cutting hardwoods, the true firs, spruce, or hemlock. All of these rot fairly quickly. (For this reason, of course, they need higher *initial* amounts of nitrogen in the process.) Way down on the list is Douglas fir, and last of all comes cedar, which is very slow to break down and toxic to seedlings in its fresh state.

Some small animals, such as rabbits, are kept without bedding. Their manure can be composted easily with vegetables and garden refuse. Poultry manure, especially chicken, is very high in available nitrogen and will compost hardwood shavings fairly quickly if mixed with kitchen and garden wastes. If pig manure is used it *must* be composted at high heat to kill parasites.

If you live near a dairy farmer who uses a solids separator—not common, unfortunately—try to obtain the solids left after the liquids have been spread. This material usually contains no bedding and is still high in nitrogen. It will compost to a usable product in six months to a year. It is rather like a silage product and, like silage, can be used directly as a mulch. Silage itself is also an excellent material for the compost pile.

Behold this compost! behold it well!
Perhaps every mite has once form'd part of a sick person—yet behold!
The grass of spring covers the prairies,
The bean bursts noiselessly through the mould in the garden,
The delicate spear of the onion pierces upward,
The apple-buds cluster together on the apple-branches,
The resurrection of the wheat appears with pale visage
    out of its graves...

—Walt Whitman

Organic Gardening

I myself garden organically. I get pretty good winter crops that way. I do this partly out of a peasant thrift and stubbornness (how could I let all that organic matter go to waste?), partly out of regard for the obvious facts of the ecosystem, and partly out of a dislike of chemicals and poisons. I get at least three cubic feet of finished compost a year from my kitchen and garden wastes; my veggies and flowers really appreciate it. I also enjoy the processes of nature far more than I do the workings of the industrial age. That is, I think it's more fun, more interesting, and less polluting to see if clovers, for instance, can manufacture the extra nitrogen we need in our gardens.

I learned to garden and farm using organic gardening methods, so when suggestions and references are given in this book, they are mostly of that sort. However, I don't want to give the impression that I *never* use manufactured chemicals; I do, if there seems to be no more satisfactory way. But it's rare, and usually restricted to ornamental crops or those few pests and diseases with which I have not yet learned to deal biologically. You *can* grow winter vegetables using chemical fertilizers and pesticides. It's done on a commercial scale, and I've heard from gardeners who do so. M. Nieuwhof, for instance, notes in *Cole Crops: Botany, Cultivation, and Utilization* that a combination of organic manure (stable, green, or compost) and chemical nitrogens often gives the best winter cabbage crops. Since he doesn't define "best," I don't know whether he includes taste, nutrition, cold-hardiness, and storage life along with size and yield. On the other hand, there are many skillful American and European commercial producers who bring off their crops using various forms of biological agriculture.

If you are currently satisfied with whatever way you are growing, well and good. Your winter vegetables will probably be no less satisfactory than your summer ones. Those who want to learn more about various biological approaches to food production should check Appendix D for further reading. I should say that there is as much sloppy, unscientific thinking and romanticism within the American organic movement as there is economically driven hype and dangerous misinformation from the chemical mainstream. (There seems to be less of this in the European movement, but perhaps I have this impression because my German and French are not as good as my English.) *You* have to practice and read with discrimination!

Varieties and Saving Seed

Even the very best microclimate, a perfect site, and great soil won't produce many winter meals if you grow summer varieties for winter cropping. Summer varieties are bred for quick production, not for staying power. Winter varieties, on the other hand, grow slowly (some are in the ground 10 months or longer), have higher dry-matter content, and have been bred to be harvested late in the fall, over the winter, or in early spring.

Winter varieties are also usually much hardier than their summer equivalents. The tendency toward slow growth, and hence high dry-matter content (which is also associated with higher nutrients), is partly responsible here. Curly Green kale is a good example of that: tough as nails but very nutritious. Broccoli is another good example. Italian Green Sprouting, DeCicco, and Waltham were once commonly available open-pollinated varieties for summer and fall cropping, though they're rarer now. If I made a later sowing than usual—July or August—these varieties produced some small winter heads. I used to do that in Seattle. But when I started gardening in the foothills out by Arlington, I found they were only hardy to about 15°F. This, of course, restricts their deep-winter use to mild areas. Purple Sprouting broccoli, on the other hand, will survive down to 5°F, which means it can be overwintered through a considerably wider range. Of course, some of that hardiness is due to Purple Sprouting's immature state as it goes into the winter; it won't attempt to form the delicate flower heads until the worst of the weather is over.

One last example: leeks. These are the quintessential winter vegetable, and yet, there are varieties of leeks bred for the fall that disintegrate with a few frosts. They are super tall with long, white shafts and thin, pale green leaves. Your true winter troopers are short, stubby, dark green, and thick leaved (again with a high dry-matter content) and will take the worst weather. Even if damaged at the core by prolonged deep frosts and desiccating wind, they will grow new centers and be harvestable again by late March.

Unfortunately, these winter-bred varieties are not all that easy to find. You usually can't just buy them from the seed racks at the local garden store, even in the maritime Northwest. Most of the vegetable breeders in the United States are busy developing varieties that can all be harvested before the dry, cold arctic air masses sweep down over field and garden. Most of the seed sales in this country are for such continental gardens; there is small economic gain in large U.S. distributors carrying special winter-bred varieties for the relatively small population of gardeners who know how to and can grow them. Because of this, most winter gardeners order their seed from a few small, northern-based U.S. and Canadian companies that carry locally adapted varieties. They also occasionally order from English, European, and Japanese companies which breed such varieties (see Appendix C for addresses).

Once you track down a few of these catalogs, how do you know which winter cabbage, leek, or cauliflower to choose for *your* garden? Since every garden and taste is different, the variety recommended by a neighbor or a seed company may not be the best one for you. And that goes for my recommendations, too. Till now I have liked Carentan leek, but you may try it along with Winter Mammoth and Alaska and come to prefer Alaska. In fact, in two years *I* might come to prefer Alaska—if it's still available! So the best way is to try out different varieties, but in a methodical manner. If you grow three varieties and one of them strikes you as pretty close to your ideal, then grow that for several years. This will give you a good idea of its abilities in different seasons and different parts of your garden. Then when you want to try new varieties, you have your "favorite" as a standard. Always grow the new and the old together, using the same sowing dates and cultural practices (fertilizing, transplanting, watering, etc.). Do this for several years. Observe the plants at as many different points in their life cycles as you can, and keep good records. You will learn much more that way.

Saving seed

Once you have settled on the varieties you like, you may want or need to save your own seed. It's extra work and takes some planning and care, plus a personal vision of what the perfect parsnip (or carrot or kale) is within any given variety. But I think in the long run it's worth it. For one thing, you can no longer count on seed companies carrying old, tried-and-true, regionally adapted favorites. The rush for "new and better" varieties (usually hybrids) is well under way, and most of the old open-pollinated types have been lost or retired to the National Seed Bank and are no longer commercially available. Concomitantly, the price of seed goes up every year along with everything else, so saving your own has distinct economic advantages.

Since 1977, when this book first went into print, an interesting metamorphosis has taken place in the seed industry. Initially, many of the more hardy and interesting varieties for winter cropping were available only from European catalogs and a few companies in the U.S. In the early eighties, there was an increase in the number of small seed companies and more interest in cool-season crops from those companies that already existed. Gardeners began to have more varieties to choose from. At the same time, though, a devastating phenomenon was taking place in the international seed market. This involved the buying up of local firms by corporate multinationals, the passing of restrictive laws concerning the ownership of genetic material—specifically hybrids—and the consequent loss of open-pollinated varieties through actual banning (loss of registration) and neglect. In other words, if the companies couldn't make any money off of an old open-pollinated variety, why should they take care of it? This is but the most recent northern-hemisphere wrinkle in the extreme loss of genetic diversity that has been going on all over the world for the last 50 years.

So what does this mean to you as a winter cropper? It means that

perhaps 90 percent of the good open-pollinated varieties are already in danger of deteriorating and thus not being offered by your local seed companies, and that the remaining varieties may go in the next five years. If this trend keeps up, you will be at the mercy of the multinationals in terms of what you can grow.

On the plus side, there are many active people, gardeners and seed people, who are working against the flow and trying to preserve and increase genetic diversity. So if you want to continue growing recommended varieties, or to try them if you are new to winter cropping, these are the people to turn to. Many of the seed companies listed in Appendix C are involved with this struggle. If you write to them, they will be more than glad to tell you which varieties they still have in stock and are able to sell or share. There is also the Seed Savers Exchange, a national group with many Northwest members; for the price of annual membership, you can join and trade seeds of their listed varieties. And in future years you can offer seeds that you yourself have grown!

Home-saved seed, if grown, collected, and stored properly, is fresher and has greater vitality. It's from *your* garden. And if you continue to save seed, the chances are, as the years go by, that your plants will be better adapted to your site and therefore healthier and more productive.

But saving seed is deceptively easy. If at the end of the winter, you

reach the end of the leek row and the five that are left are beginning to bolt, you might be tempted to say, "Oh, well, I'll save them for seed." Doing it that way, you get a pig in a poke. You should start the process by reading what you can about saving and storing seed (see Appendix D). Then carefully consider what to start with.

Let's use leeks as an example again. Start the process in the fall by going over the leeks and picking the ones that you think are best. Mark these so you won't eat them by mistake. Since leeks are cross-pollinated, you will want to save a fair number, say 10 or 15. (This will give you more seed than you need, but you can always share it.)

Watch how they do through the winter weather. If their performance is as good as their looks, then save them for seed. If not, then rogue them out ruthlessly! Because of weed and cultivation problems, it is best to transplant them in late February to a spot on the edge of the garden, or even to a flower bed where they can be admired. Plants in the process of going to seed are usually wider and taller than when in the vegetative state. They often need to be staked. In late summer when you can see the dry black seeds within the husks of the flowers, you can shake them out into a basket or bag and bring them into the house for final drying. And there you are with your own leek seed!

Timing

The question of when to sow different plants so that they are in a proper condition for fall, winter, or early spring harvest is a complex one. Each winter variety has its own requirements. Parsnips and leeks, typical slow-growing biennials, must be sown early in the spring to have time to reach maturity; spinach and Chinese cabbage, typical winter annuals, need to be sown late enough in the summer so they won't bolt, but early enough to put on good growth. Kales, carrots, and beets, faster-growing biennials, are sown in June and July.

The chart "Timing for Winter Crop Sowing" gives an idea of the general timing needed for cold-hardy crops. You will notice that some of the most valuable winter vegetables are sown in July and August, which is already a busy time with harvest, vacations, and other summer activities. But if you want these crops, you will need to plan ahead and allot time to prepare the beds, sow the seed, and keep the plants watered and weeded. To simplify your first season, choose only a *few* of the more basic types to start with. After you get the hang of it, you can expand! Remember that you can cut out *some* of the preserving of summer crops; winter cabbages and leeks mean fewer frozen beans or servings of corn are needed for winter meals.

Another aspect to be considered in the timing of winter crops is your climate zone. This is determined by your latitude, topography, proximity to large bodies of water, and general weather patterns. The best and most complete discussion of zones for the western U.S. is in the *Sunset New Western Garden Book*. It covers the area from California up to the northern border of Washington. I only wish the authors had extended their map another 30 miles north to include the Fraser River Valley of British

Timing for Cool Season Crop Sowing and Transplanting

In cold frames

Early beets	February, July
Bok choy	February, March
Burdock	March, April
Fall/winter cabbage tribe	April*; **June**
Carrots	January, February
Coriander	February, March
Cress	February, March
Favas	January, February, March
Spring kales	January
Leeks	March, April; **May, June**
Early lettuce	January, February, March
Mustards	January, February, March
Parsnips	March, April
Rocket	January, February, March
Salsify	March, April
Spinach	January, February, March
Turnips	February

In flats

Winter cauliflower	June; **July**
Celeriac	March, April; **May, June**
Celery	March, April; **May, June**
Chicory	July 15
Chinese cabbage	July
Corn salad	August
Endive	July
Favas	October
Florence fennel	July
Garlic	October
Curly kales	June, July
Keeper beets	May, June
Keeper carrots	July
Kohlrabi	June
Fall lettuce	July, August
Overwintering lettuce	September, October
Overwintering onions	July 15–August 15
Winter radish	August
Rutabagas	July
Siberian kale	July
Spinach	August, September, October
Swiss chard	May, June
Turnips	July

In cold frames

Cabbage	September
Coriander	September
Corn salad	October
Lettuce	September, October
Mustards	September, October
Radish	September
Rocket	September, October
Spinach	September

*The timing for sowing the fall/winter crop of the cabbage tribe will depend upon root fly egg-laying in your district. See Sharecroppers for how to determine this. Transplanting is approximately a month later.

Note: Sowing times only for cool-season crop. Many crops can also be planted in spring/summer months for summer crop, e.g. lettuce, coriander, cabbage, etc. Months that appear in **boldface** type indicate transplanting times.

Columbia, which is the last substantial agricultural valley before Alaska. This general area includes the city of Vancouver and Vancouver Island and is mostly zones four and five. A great deal of winter cropping is possible here and is practiced both commercially and by home gardeners.

Knowing your climate zone will give you a *general* idea of what you can grow and when you can sow it. But within each zone, though the temperature may be similar at any given point of the year, there will often be differences in rainfall, cloud cover, and wind. For example, zone five on the coast of Washington is a lot wetter and windier than zone five along Puget Sound or in the San Juan Islands. Coastal growers might be troubled more by rotting of early seeds and, later, of mature plants. Their cold frames should be designed to protect against frequent rainfall and high wind. In these coastal gardens, although the winter frosts are less severe, the average summer temperature is cooler and plants need a longer time to reach maturity.

Inland in zone four, the frosts are harder, last later into the spring, and begin earlier in the fall. But, at least at lower elevations, the days are warmer in the summer, so plants can come to maturity as soon as plants closer to water in the same zone, or even sooner. At higher elevations the seasons are shorter, and the frosts and snow cover are greater, making a climate suited to only the quickest and hardiest of winter crops.

Oregon has a similar east/west pattern. The slightly warmer Willamette Valley allows for crops to be sown a week or two earlier in the spring than in northern Washington and a week or two later in the summer and fall, but coast and foothill gardens will have their own timings. South, the Rogue Valley district is a hodgepodge of microclimates created by diverse weather patterns and topography. If all this seems confusing to you, don't despair! You can probably figure out what to do from your own experiments and with the aid of neighboring gardeners.

In fact, wherever you live, there are probably local resources. Lively extension agents or Master Gardeners may be helpful. Local chapters of Tilth (see Appendix C) and other gardening groups may have experimented with extending the season of crop production. Gardening books written by local authors are always useful. Last but not least, seed companies often explain in their catalogs when they sow certain winter crops. The way to adjust those timings to your site is to make a few succession plantings and *keep good notes*. If you do this, in three or four years you will have a good sense of your winter crop timing.

One thing that confused *me* a lot when I first started winter gardening was that English seed catalogs suggested sowing various crops—brassicas and lettuces, for instance—a lot earlier than I was used to. When I tried their timing, it didn't work out for me. The best I could figure out was that I was just enough farther south and the climate was just enough warmer for the earlier dates not to work.

When you crop year-round, you put seeds in the ground eight months of the year. Keeping seeds and sowing dates straight can be wearisome, and it helps to be organized. If your seed packets are in an alphabetical file, you won't have to spend hours finding the winter lettuce or the kale seed. A list of sowing dates on your refrigerator will remind you when to plant what. I have taken to keeping a small cardboard box in an obvious place filled with the seeds for that month. (The boxes from the seed companies are often the right size and shape.) Here I also store tags and a marking crayon. If you take notes you can keep them in the box, too. Make life easy for yourself. Doing it this way may seem a bit mechanical, but I find that having this basic information on a chart rests my brain. It allows me more time to think about the other variables of gardening, like what the weather's doing, or even what's going on in the rest of my life!

Watching the weather provides another guide for when to sow and transplant your vegetables. Scan the horizon frequently. Keep records (mental or on your calendar) of when the weather did what. Observe the length of wet and dry spells. Does the phase of the moon have an effect

in your area? (In northwest Washington, it often clears up or stops rain-
ing a few days before full moon.) Does it seem as though it's going to
be an early, dry spring? A late, wet one? Place your bets and gamble
in the garden.

Waiting

Winter is shorter when you know a garden
and can still pull beets in early December.
Even after everything's turned under
long nights are hours of rest, not death,
earned sleep after the land's labor

when kitchen tables bear seed packets,
almanacs, sketches,
when conversation
conjures up a tangled trellis of peas
before the first one plumps in a furrow.

That day apple twigs are already knobbier,
crocus tips slice old mulch,
                    February
is already spring.

Robins watch the hoe.

—Jody Aliesan

Winter Gardening Mechanics

Starting out

When you overwinter vegetables for the first time, it's best to begin with just a few of the easiest and very hardiest. The "Beginner's Easy and Very Hardy List" will give you some idea of what to start with. I have arranged the vegetables by sowing date so you can plan ahead and fit them into your spring and summer sowing schedule.

If you live in an area that gets deep frosts and extended cold spells, you can keep a pile of hay by the garden for mulching. Wherever you live, if the temperature drops below 25°F and the forecast is for the cold to continue, mulch as soon as you can. By mulching over unfrozen soil, you have the best chance of keeping the plants in good condition. Unfrozen soil also makes harvesting roots and leeks easier. All the vegetables listed have, in my experience, survived to 5°F with severe winds. Production, of course, stops until the weather improves, maybe February or March, but you are still *way* ahead of what any spring planting could do.

Beginner's Easy and Very Hardy List

Month for sowing	Vegetable
April	Jerusalem artichokes Leeks Parsley Parsnips Salsify Scallions
May–June	Kale Savoy cabbage Swiss chard
August–September	Corn salad* Overwintering onions Spinach* Lettuce*

---

*These are more productive if covered during December–March, unless the winter is very mild. During cold spells, all three will survive temperatures as low as -2°F if covered with a material like Reemay underneath a cold frame.

Spacing

The spacing of hardy crops sometimes differs from that of the summer varieties of the same vegetable. An example is cauliflower. In northern latitudes, fall and overwintering cauliflowers benefit from a spacing of 18 to 30 inches apart in the row or bed, whereas their summer counterparts can get by with 12 inches.

Naturally, spacing is somewhat dependent on soil fertility—the richer the soil the closer the plants, up to a point—but in general, plants that overwinter have time for more root growth and will produce a bigger plant if allowed. If you have a small family or a small garden and don't want huge leeks or monstrous spring cauliflowers, then you are better off to space a little tighter. Vegetables that are susceptible to leaf rot, such as lettuce, benefit from the passage of air between the plants. Even plants such as the dwarf winter romaines, which *could* be grown cheek by jowl, should be given a little extra room.

Beds

I am of the opinion that winter crops, as well as most of the smaller summer ones, should be grown in a wide row or raised bed. There are several reasons for this. First, you get higher production per unit of ground. Second, you are not trampling the soil around the roots. Third, the larger surface area of beds helps to warm the soil. And fourth, because the paths sink and compact as you walk on them, drainage off the beds improves.

Several modern books discuss this "new" intensive bed method (see Appendix D), but actually it has been in use for hundreds of years, in both Asia and Europe. J.K. Bleasdale and D.J. Salter, in *Know and Grow Vegetables,* report that this method was used to grow vegetables in England before the Industrial Revolution lured the market-garden laborers (mainly women and children) into the new factories. Then the farmers began to use the recently developed horse-drawn cultivation machines, and widely spaced single rows became the standard. Gardeners soon copied this, and then it became the norm. Today, some commercial growers are reversing this process, taking their cue from the successes of bed gardeners and working out ways to create and weed beds with machines.

Rotation

Crop rotation is an accepted practice with experienced gardeners and farmers. The main idea is simple: don't grow the same crop, or species in the same family, in the same area two years in a row. This prevents concentrations of pests and diseases and makes better use of the soil's resources. Because gardeners have been rotating crops in so many different situations for so long, there are many different systems and opinions about them.

Typical 3-year Rotation

Add organic manure	Add fertilizer and lime	Add fertilizer
Group A. Other crops	Group B. Brassicas	Group C. Root crops
Peas	Cabbage	Carrots
Beans	Cauliflower	Parsnips
Onions	Brussels sprouts	Beets
Leeks	Broccoli	Potatoes
Lettuce	Swedes	Tomatoes
Celery	Turnips	
Group sequence 1st year ABC	2nd year BCA	3rd year CAB

A typical English garden rotation system from *Know and Grow Vegetables 2*.

It's probably best to read about rotations and then devise one of your own. Year-round growing does make this process slightly more complex, but not unbearably so. I find it rather like three-dimensional tic-tac-toe or chess. To keep it all clear, I just make a map of the garden every year and try not to put a main crop (cabbage family, onion family, roots, corn, tomatoes, etc.) in the same place more than once every three years. (Four is better, if you can manage it.) I also pay attention to the needs of each crop and try to accommodate them: high pH, low pH, high fertility, medium fertility, and so on. In fact, what crop follows what can be based on those criteria to some degree.

Don't confuse crop rotation with succession planting, which is the planting of several different crops (say, of lettuce) within the same season.

Winter weeds

One result of year-round cropping is a whole new set of weeds. When you till your garden in October and put it to bed with a green manure for the winter, you don't have to worry about perennial and winter annual weeds. One fine day in March, you till up the whole thing; when it's rotted down enough, you till again, and then you start to sow summer crops. Maybe you encounter some quackgrass or a few thistles, but mostly you are dealing with summer annuals such as lamb's-quarters, pigweed, and barnyard grass.

But if you have six to 10 vegetable crops that are ready at different times from January through May, you can develop spotty areas of weeds that will overwinter just as happily as your vegetables: cress, dock, chickweed, groundsel, various grasses, dandelions, mallow, cranesbill. . . . I could go on, but I won't. One way to deal with this is with a thick mulch of hay, sawdust, cardboard, or some such. Another is to make sure that the late-cropping vegetables, such as cauliflowers, leeks, lettuce, and spinach, are all together in one spot. During the early fall and early spring it pays to weed the beds and paths frequently. Then in late May when the winter crops are done, you have just one big area that you can cultivate all at once. Sow it to green manure for the early part of the summer. If you are fallowing, you can make this your fallow area.

Picking Your Produce and Eating It

Harvesting winter crops is pretty straightforward. There are only a few things to remember. First, don't plant more than you can eat. You will have to allow some extra for frost damage, but not that much more. Second, learn to pick crops in their season. Cabbages are a good example. If you love savoys and have four different varieties due to crop in early fall, late fall, midwinter, and late winter, make sure you follow the pattern. Because they are faster growing, the fall ones will be overmature by Christmas and will suffer damage from heavy frosts and high rainfall. When you go out into the garden to get one for supper, look over the selection and take the poorest-looking one first; the healthier, more vigorous specimens will last longer.

With the winter annuals, such as spinach, lettuce, and corn salad, that overwinter in the rosette form, pick the outer leaves rather than taking whole plants. This stimulates the growth of new leaves from the core. Lettuce especially needs to have its old, disease-prone leaves removed even if you don't eat them. By late March, or early April in the north, you will start to have an abundance of lettuce and other rosette plants, and your spring sowings will be coming on soon. Then you can shift over to taking whole plants before they bolt to seed.

If you live in an area subject to frequent freezing spells, try not to pick from your garden when the plants are frozen solid unless you are going to cook and eat them right away. Otherwise they'll likely rot in your refrigerator. Do your harvesting when the mercury is above 32°F, and collect enough to last you for a while. The salad greens keep well in plastic bags, parsley bunches in a small glass of water, and cabbages in any cool place. Don't overdo it, though; vitamin levels drop daily in storage.

When you go out into the garden after a freeze or a bout of snow, it sometimes takes a little imagination to recognize a healthy red-cabbage salad under the frosted, slimy leaves, or a stir-fry in March's weird, elongated, almost-flowering Brussels sprouts. But just because supermarkets don't usually sell flowers for eating doesn't mean they aren't delicious. As for the cabbages, you can peel back the slimy leaves and throw them out just as easily as the produce manager does.

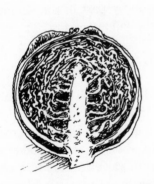

Once you get to the kitchen many of the winter-hardy plants may be new to you and your family, so it's important to seek recipes that show them at their best. If you overcook them or yield to the temptation to always serve them in the same way, they will quickly become boring. That path leads back to the supermarket bins of expensive, unvital vegetables. L. D. Hills has some good recipes, and Rombauer's *Joy of Cooking,* that marvelous kitchen standby, even has salsify recipes! And new cookbooks arrive all the time. Marian Morash's *The Victory Garden Cookbook* is such a one. Morash's husband, Russell, produced the television show "Crockett's Victory Garden," and the book reflects the couple's gardening and culinary expertise. Organized by its vegetable ingredients, it has 6½ pages on celeriac alone!

Substitution works well, too. If you can't find something new to do with kale, and it's all you've got left in the garden, just think of a gourmet sauce that's good over some other vegetable and use that.

Self-confidence

You might at first doubt that self-confidence is as vital a component of winter gardening as site, climate, or soil, but it certainly is. I became aware of this when I first started visiting other people's gardens. They would usually spend the first few minutes apologizing for the terrible condition of their plot, excusing the state of the broccoli, and pardoning the peas.

Many had spent the day before my arrival weeding as if I were their relative come to inspect for dust on the mantel, assuming for some strange reason that I never had weeds in my garden, or that my broccoli never failed and my peas never shriveled. After I wrote the first edition of *Winter Gardening,* another thing began to happen. People would say how much they enjoyed the book but then shamefacedly admit that they weren't growing very many winter vegetables. Well, that's okay! I assume that the *first* principle of gardening is that it is an art devoted to the feeding of a family *by* that family, and that, while you may or may not appreciate the aesthetics or routines of another's garden, if it feeds them, then how it looks hardly matters.

You should have the self-confidence to do whatever is right for you. For example, you may have decided that Brussels sprouts are too much trouble, that *you* don't want to stand outside bent over in the rain for 10 minutes cutting those little knobs off the main stem and then spend an additional 20 minutes in the kitchen pruning and cleaning them before cooking. In the same space you might have a savoy cabbage, equally hardy, that you could pick with one fell swoop of your knife and devote but three minutes to cutting up and sautéing for dinner. But if your neighbor loves Brussels sprouts and hates savoys, who's to argue?

Another example comes out of one of the nicest things that has happened in the last few years, the development of the "salad" movement. In our neck of the woods, Mark Musick and Robin Stern of Tilth did a lot of the introductory work; in England, it was Joy Larkcom. As a result of this, people are picking small leaves of unusual greens and edible flowers for exotic salads. They are not only gorgeous, but delicious. Many of the varieties are cool-season crops, and it has been a delight to me to see some of these used in ways I never would have predicted. In fact, many varieties that I had rejected or ignored are being used—a lesson in itself about the merit of doing your own experiments instead of taking someone else's words as gospel.

Indeed, I have sometimes thought that gardening is rather like bushwhacking in the mountains. There you are, contour map in hand, gear on your back, setting off from the trailhead. Every once in a while as you walk along you consult the map to see what that peak over there is, whether this stream has a name, and of course, how much farther you have to go. Then you come around a point of land and decide you'd like to try a shortcut. It's at this point that you're on your own for a while. For a contour map is pretty general, and at 80-foot intervals it's not going to tell you much about the details. Once you've deumbilicalized yourself from the trail, you have to rely on your senses. You are right there on the mountainside, with every stone and boulder, lichen and fir, flowers at your feet and an ice peak up ahead. If you can relax enough, you and the mountainside become the trail, your own trail, but also only one of the many trails in that field.

Alpine bushwhacking is, of course, easy because of the view. Bushwhacking down below in the firs and brush is another matter. Winter gardening is still pretty easy because the view is open. There aren't a lot of books and experts, as there are in summer gardening, growing up like firs and bushes to obscure your view.

Of course, most people think I'm an expert by this time. And certainly I have filled all these pages with what I think I know. But it's just a contour map, and *you* will encounter the details. Also, it's hard to write about what I don't know when I don't know it yet! So have faith in your own abilities, and in the plants, and just go ahead and experiment.

> *You should not lose your self-sufficient state of mind. This does not mean a closed mind, but actually an empty mind and a ready mind. If your mind is empty, it is always ready for anything; it is open to everything. In the beginner's mind there are many possibilities; in the expert's mind there are few.*
>
> —Suzuki Roshi

CLOCHES
AND FRAMES

Introduction

Some of the best of the cold-hardy crops benefit from protection by frames or cloches. In the fall these include lettuce, spinach, rocket, the immature overwintering European cabbages, and the leafy Asian brassicas. The very-early spring plantings of peas, lettuce, carrots, beets, spinach, turnips, potatoes, and members of the cabbage tribe (broccoli, cabbage, cauliflower, etc.) can all be advanced about a month by the use of glass. A bit later on, the seed bed for leeks and annual flowers can be covered to advantage, and frames can be used during the summer on heat-loving crops such as tomatoes, peppers, and melons.

But like vegetable varieties, frames must be matched to the climate. Most Americans think of a cold frame as the high-walled sort, popular in continental climates, that remain in a fixed spot in the garden. While these are good for starting flats of hardy plants or hardening off tender ones, they are not really suited to gardening year-round in a maritime climate.

To my mind the best frames are *modular* ones that can be easily moved from one part of the garden to another to follow your successions and rotation of crops. In some gardens I made the beds in the part of the garden that got most of the winter crops the length of five of my frames, so that I could cover a whole bed without any wasted space. This also helped me to estimate how much to plant: four frames of spinach, one of lettuce, one of turnips and other greens, etc. Very handy!

A reliable *venting system* is another necessity for frames in our climate. Ventilation is far more important than weatherproofing in a maritime climate. If you look at a cold-frame design from an East Coast or Midwestern book, you will encounter all sorts of tricks—insulation, double glazing, heat storage—that, as far as I can see, are unnecessary or even harmful here. We have far more cloud cover and much warmer winters. If you were to grow lettuce at our low light levels, and in the high-temperature, high-humidity environment of an airtight frame, you would get leggy, weak plants and lots of fungal growth. Cold frames suited to continental climates have to combat desiccating low temperatures, but they often have fair light levels, even at the winter solstice, due to the many sunny days and the highly reflective snow cover.

In mild falls it is important to leave cold frames holding lettuce and spring cabbages open. Light levels in November and December are quite low, and if the days are warm, covered plants will put on too much weak, sappy growth. If a hard freeze comes in late December or early January, the plants will be too tender and succumb to frost, even with the covers back on. If you live in a very cold area, it's a good idea to have some old rugs or mats to place on the frames during very hard freezes. A thick hay mulch will work too, though it is more of a bother.

Another important reason to have permanently opened vents, or some automatic system set to a certain temperature, is the uncertainty of our weather. On those winter days when the sun comes out for an hour or so, temperatures can rise much more quickly in an enclosed space than outside. Since the average cloudy winter day in the maritime Northwest runs about 45°F, it doesn't take too long in the sun to reach a point at which the plants, with their roots in cold soil, will suffer from evaporation stress.

Old books on frame gardening say that most venting should happen from the top of the frame or cloche to avoid a draft over the plants. An exception is on clear, freezing mornings, when venting from the bottom allows a slow warmup and lets the plants thaw more gently. If you have tunnel cloches, you should vent from the top, never the ends, to avoid disastrous breezes through the tunnel. Because heat rises, top venting also utilizes natural convection. If possible, place your frames crossways to the wind so the area behind them is also sheltered.

Having said all this about ventilation, I must point out that there are forms of covers for which ventilation in the depths of winter (December through February) is mostly unnecessary. These are *translucent* covers rather than transparent ones, which come in plastic or fiberglass. The plastic ones, usually sold through commercial catalogs, are among the best winter covers. They are more flexible than regular plastic in cold weather (and thus last longer) and are not so easily destroyed by high winds. As long as they are held down by wires *over* the plastic as well as underneath, they will stand up very well. A translucent fabric especially designed for greenhouses and tunnels is Fabrene, a flexible fiber-bonded product (see Appendix C for one source, Stocote Products). I haven't tried the *slit* row covers for the winter months, as I didn't think they would be warm or dry enough. Corrugated fiberglass can be obtained from building centers.

Another aspect of frame growing is the importance of watering. Many frames completely exclude rain, and even narrow cloches, which allow some moisture to seep into the soil beneath the covers, can have problems with very dry surface soil after a couple of weeks with low rainfall. If this happens in the spring, young plants of lettuce and bok choy, peas, and so on should be watered as needed. Fall plantings are not in as much danger, since they usually have bigger root systems, and the soil is wet by the time they are covered. But, even so, they should be watched.

Almost all frames will need some form of *guying*, or fastening against the wind. Few things are as disturbing as finding torn plastic, frames, and broken glass all over your garden after a stormy night.

Appendix D lists several good books, articles, and pamphlets on growing under frames. You can learn a fair amount from them, but you will have to work out your own schedule of what to grow and when to cover it.

Following are notes on some of the types of frames and cloches that I have found useful (or not) in recent years.

Walls and terraces

The easiest place to create a warm microclimate is a south-facing wall or terrace. Either can have old window frames leant against it to shelter plants. A disadvantage of walls is that after the spring equinox they lose light as the sun begins to rise and set to the north. This makes walls best for the low-growing, quick winter annuals such as corn salad, lettuce, spinach, and some tender herbs such as rosemary. If the wall belongs to a building with broad eaves this site will also be quite dry—a plus in winter, a disadvantage in summer.

If your land has a considerable slope, terraces can be useful, as they are well drained but more exposed to sun and rainfall. Remember that the warmest spot is right against the riser, so don't put your path there.

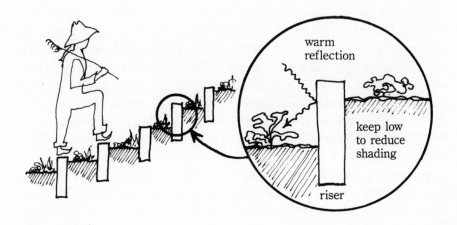

Cloches

The word "cloche," which comes from the French for "bell," originally referred to the bell-shaped jars that were used as hot caps to put over
tender plants early in the year to protect them from frost. The term expanded in meaning to include many different sizes and shapes of glass
structures for protecting individual plants in a row or whole row (a barn
or tent cloche). Now some are available in fiberglass and other long-lasting
synthetics, but they are quite expensive—handy if you have the money,
though. Others you can make yourself for a small investment.

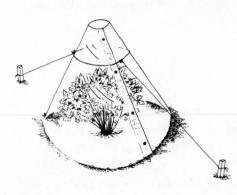

Fiberglass cone: A pattern for
this is available from Solar Survival (see Appendix C). It is handy
to put over individual herbs or
heat-loving plants such as egg-
plants, of which you may have
only a few. Good for forcing rhu-
barb when covered with a dark
cloth. A more modern version of
this is the "wall of water" device
sold in some gardening-supply
catalogs.

Bottle: Cut the bottoms off used plastic gallon jugs and make temporary
cloches for the earliest brassicas and cucurbits. Most are too small and

opaque to be good for overwintering plants. When you use them on brassicas, cover the top opening with a screen to keep pests out. Watch for overheating and mildew.

Corrugated fiberglass: I haven't used this, but others seem to like it. You will have to devise your own ventilation system. I would opt for cutting a series of small holes in the top. (The vents could be taped over during the coldest or rainiest times.) One real draw- back is that the whole structure must be removed when you want to work on the plants.

Cloche wires and clips: Cloches made from panes of glass and specially constructed wires were developed by an Englishman named Chase in 1912. Modified only slightly since then, they have remained deservedly popular with gardeners and commercial

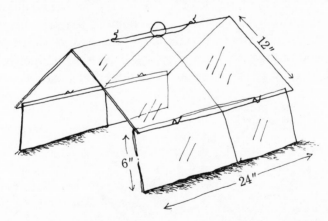

growers. When properly put together, each cloche is rigid and can be moved as a unit. The top pane of glass can be removed to work on the crops underneath. The maximum size available is 23 inches wide by 24 inches long. I don't know of any U.S. outlet; see Appendix C for the ad- dress of Picken & Son Ltd., a British supplier for Chase cloche wires.

A more recent development is the use of plastic clips instead of wires to hold the glass. These do not hold the panes of glass rigid, and they're susceptible to wind damage. Furthermore, there is no quick and effi- cient way to remove the front pane when you want to weed, water, or pick crops. I don't recommend them.

Caterpillars, pods, and pup tents

In the early '80s, the National Center for Appropriate Technology tested and publicized various types of cold frames. It awarded grants to regional groups to test old types, develop new ones, devise planting schemes to use in them, and let the gardening public know about them. While many of the new cold frames are ingenious, none of them to my mind and experience is as useful and simple as the old types.

Caterpillar: Constructed of wire or PVC pipe and heavy-duty polyethylene sheeting. Cheap and easy to make, caterpillars are well suited to wide rows or beds. They don't hold up too well in wind, so they're best for protected city lots and summer use. You can make a crawl-in size at extra expense.

Tunnels: A variation of the above are the tunnels that I mentioned earlier. For these you must get some 9-gauge wire cut into lengths approximately four feet long. They are bent into a semi-circle and stuck into the ground on either side of the bed. I try not to make these hoops any taller than 18 inches at the highest point so that they present a low profile to the winter winds. If your soil is very hard or rocky, you might have to bend the wires so that they will enter the soil more shallowly. Over this, place your row-cover fabric and tie it to stakes on either side.

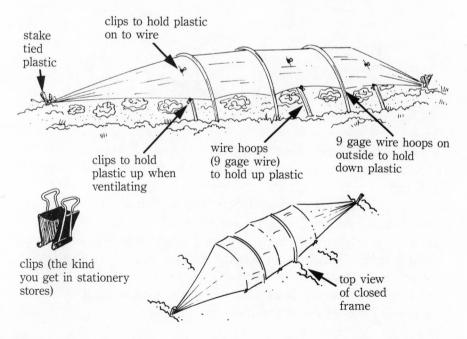

stake
tied
plastic

clips to hold plastic
on to wire

clips to hold
plastic up when
ventilating

wire hoops
(9 gage wire)
to hold up plastic

9 gage wire hoops on
outside to hold
down plastic

clips (the kind
you get in stationery
stores)

top view
of closed
frame

In the winter months, I tie a string from one stake and loop it around each inside hoop till I reach the stake at the other end. This acts as a guy to hold the hoops up against the force of the wind, snow, and rain. Another series of wires on top of the row cover holds down the fabric. This is a fairly secure system and will *usually* last the winter. At this writing, this is my preferred system for protecting both rows and plug flats for the spring starts.

Pod: This is a tunnel formed of fiberglass with solid plywood ends. It is sturdy and able to withstand winter winds, and not *too* heavy to carry around. Ventilation and access to plants are problems. All things considered, I wouldn't build one for my garden.

Pup tent: A wooden frame built in the shape of a low tent. The sides are covered with fiberglass or poly sheeting. They do not lift off, so ventilation and access to plants are difficult. Some commercial variations of these, built with poly frames, are available in gardening catalogs. They look like they would be good for fall and spring as long as they were guyed in windy districts.

Old window frames

If you have a source of old wood or aluminum window sashes, you can use them to construct two sorts of frames. They are cheap, easy to put together, modular (if the windows are the same size), stable when guyed, and easily vented. These frames will take crops through some of the coldest winters we get. They also provide easy access to crops beneath them. The one disadvantage is that when these frames are set up in the tent form, the plants closest to the edge are a bit crowded by the lower slope

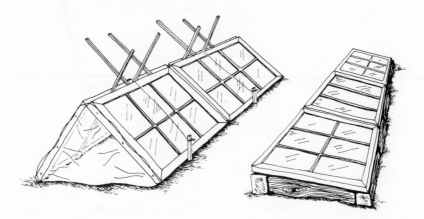

of the glass. If the panes break you can reglaze them with fiberglass. Fiberglass panes are lighter, though, and always need guying systems in windy areas.

Dutch lights

In the nineteenth century, French and then Dutch market gardeners evolved very practical and inexpensive modular structures for frame gardening. Except for floating row covers, they are probably the best thing around for commercial producers. They are certainly more enduring, and you don't send anything to the dump at the end of the year, which you do with the row covers. I suppose that soon row covers will come in biodegradable forms, and then they will beat the Dutch light for the warmer months of the year—but maybe not for winter use.

Dutch lights consist of a framework of low wooden rims, or boards, with those on the north side a few inches taller than those on the south. These boards support long panes of glass, which are fitted into treated or painted frames held in place by glazier's points or blocks of wood. No putty is used, as it does not stand up well to the weather and makes glass replacement an unnecessarily tedious job.

Access is achieved by removing the cover entirely, or by sliding it over on top of its neighbor. To ventilate, prop up the top or leeward side of the frame. Minor disadvantages are that the southern rim blocks some of the low winter sun, and unless the frame is narrow front to back, access to the plants in the rear is a bit difficult. European gardeners use boards

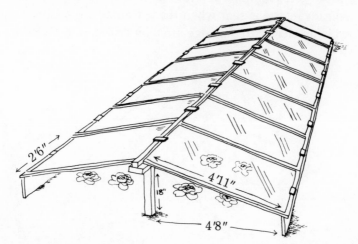

Double dutch lights. Ends are closed off with boards held in place with stakes.

between the rows or propped up over the plants to lean on as they do their work. Dutch lights are built in single or double form. I saw these still in use in Europe in 1985. In the organic farm garden at Washington's Evergreen State College, they found glass covers to be far too heavy for the large double frames they made, and so they used corrugated fiberglass. These are very successful, but are not moved around the garden.

Hot beds

A hot bed is any kind of large cold frame with a manure-filled pit under it. The manure decomposes and in the process generates heat and carbon dioxide, both useful to the plants in the bed. Horse manure is the best to use, as it provides the longest lasting, most even heat.

Opinions differ as to the amount or depth of manure required to generate heat. Several people have reported to me that they don't get any heat unless they use three feet of manure. This seems like rather a lot. *Intensive Culture of Vegetables: The French System,* a very good book written in 1913 by a commercial English gardener, calls for 10 inches of well-packed horse manure and straw, *half old, half new.* The manure must be moist so that bacterial action can take place.

I have used as little as eight inches of horse manure under my melon beds, but I didn't get much extra heat—maybe an extra 5°F. Friends who used two feet under a walk-in frame in Seattle got considerable heat in January.

Six to eight inches of soil goes on top of the manure, to raise the bed to its normal level. You can then sow seeds or put in transplants.

SHARECROPPERS

Introduction

I haven't encountered too many pests or diseases during the winter. Slugs, mice, and rot are the main exceptions. But for the slow plants, ones that have to grow all summer to produce in the winter, there are indeed some formidable sharecroppers. "Take-alls" might be a better term!

When dealing with any pest, I think it's useful to take the time to understand the organism, its life cycle, and its place in the local ecosystem. If you just run for the Raid can, *or* the rotenone, you risk breeding resistant pests. Even worse, you never come to understand *why* you have this pest and *if* you can change your gardening habits to reduce its predation to an insignificant level.

One way of dealing with pests in a coordinated manner is through a set of procedures referred to as "integrated pest management" (IPM). What follows is a short outline of this method; for a longer discussion, read Helga Olkowski's *Management of the Pest Garden Slug.*

The first step in IPM is to systematically check out what is happening. What sort of damage is occurring and on which plants? Is it happening at night or in the day? Can you see the culprits, or just their effect? (Perhaps a neighbor, your local extension agent, or a Master Gardener can aid in identifying the organisms.) Will your yield be decreased? How much? This observation is called *monitoring.*

Once you have zeroed in on the pest organism, look at your yard and garden and figure out where the pest is hiding and if any of your gardening habits—or your ornamental vegetation—encourage or discourage the pest. Neatness and cleanliness are often next to pestlessness. Steps you take to change any of these factors to discourage the pest are *habitat manipulation.*

Sometimes *when* you plant a crop or *how* you take care of it will increase or decrease the damage. So changes in your gardening patterns— *cultural controls*—are a possibility. An example is waiting to transplant sensitive brassicas until most of the cabbage flies have stopped laying eggs.

Encouraging pest predators—*biological controls*—is helpful, too, though this is often difficult and expensive for home gardeners. In the maritime Northwest, we have many imported pests whose original habitats and predators were left behind. There may be useful local predators, though, and you can spend some time observing them. Birds and syrphid flies belong in this category. Importing predators is often useless, as they simply migrate out of your garden. But you should learn to recognize your local ones. With reading and observation, you can learn to create habitats for the native predators you want to have around. See Appendix D for some useful titles.

You can also try *barriers* to keep the pest organism from getting to the crop. What method you use depends upon whether it flies, crawls, burrows, or slimes. Setting *traps* is often effective.

Finally, there is the use of *poisons,* whether "organic" botanicals, such as rotenone, pyrethrum, and derris, or the numerous and usually (though not always) more toxic "chemical" ones.

The IPM method takes a little extra time and attention on your part. It is not an instant solution. But then, instant solutions often have disastrous side effects. Better to observe carefully and continually, gather information, generate solutions, and implement them thoughtfully—and only to the extent necessary.

I should add here that there are organic growers, theorists, and writers who believe that pests do not attack healthy plants. They say that if the soil is in good tilth or balance, garden conditions are right, and the gardener is not guilty of mismanagement, a clean, productive garden will result with few, if any, problems. I myself think that's a complex set of ifs.

Certainly healthy, living soil and healthy plants are the best defense against disease and perhaps even predation, but often as not one inherits a garden site that is way out of balance. And we have little control over the practices of our neighbors, let alone those in adjacent sections of the county or city. Further, it takes some time and a lot of work to develop garden patterns that work well in a given site. So don't despair or feel guilty or inadequate if you have some problems in your garden.

Cabbage aphid (Aphididae spp.)

Cabbage aphids are gray, mealy-looking critters that overwinter in colonies on the underside of leaves of mature brassica plants. In the early summer—May—right after you've set out your transplants, the mature ones fly around looking for hosts. If they land on the young brassicas, they crawl down into the center of the plants and start feeding and hatching new aphids. This causes the leaves to warp and curl around them so they are hard to eradicate. If not stopped, they can permanently damage the plants.

Cabbage aphids are parasitized by tiny braconid wasps, whose offspring feed within the bodies of the young, turning them into little golden mummies. If you see a high proportion of mummies to feeding aphids, you can assume that control is under way. Then you need only give the seedlings or plants a boost with seaweed or manure teas or a mulch of partly aged manure. Other helpful predators of aphids are lacewing larvae, lady beetles and their larvae, and syrphid fly larvae. As the adults of the last of these prefer to feed on flowers of the Umbelliferae, or carrot family, I make sure to let some umbellifers, such as parsley, dill, and coriander, go to flower for them.

If you regularly overwinter kale, Purple Sprouting broccoli, and hardy cauliflowers, the chances are strong that the plants are sheltering overwintering colonies of mature aphids or their eggs. You should either clear out these plants by the middle of May or spray them with a solution of Safer's Insecticidal Soap, which has worked well for me. Safer's Insecticidal Soap is registered as an insecticide and is available in garden centers and greenhouse-supply stores. Basic H, liquid Joy, liquid Ivory, and vegetable soaps that are often found in co-ops and health-food stores are not registered; however, they do work! One just isn't allowed by law to recommend them. Some detergents are phytotoxic (bad for plants), so it's best not to use them.

Reliable sources tell me that malathion, though hardly desirable, is far less toxic in its immediate effects to you and the predators than the often-recommended homemade, but acutely toxic, nicotine spray. Nonetheless, a 1983 broadcast of *All Things Considered* on National Public Radio reported studies on the long-term effects of malathion and similar poisons on brain-wave activity that make me want to stick with soap.

If your new plants become infested with aphids during the summer months, you can wipe them off with your fingers and just spray a little soap solution down into the center right around the growing tip. Protecting young cabbage plants by this method takes some persistence, but it's worth it. I have lost all too many of my winter brassicas due to inattention! Some hot, dry summers encourage aphids and you have to guard even the older plants. Leaves and stalks damaged by aphids are susceptible to mold in later rainy weather.

Cabbage loopers *Trichoplusia ni*
Imported cabbageworms *Pieris rapae*

The larvae of a white butterfly, the imported cabbageworm, and of a brownish moth, the cabbage looper, both eat holes in the leaves of cabbages and sometimes broccoli. They are often a problem in western Washington.

There are at least two and sometimes three generations of butterflies each year. The first generation, in the spring, is not as intense as the late-summer ones. Though the moth goes through several generations, I have observed its larvae only in the late summer. Both kinds of larvae can be picked off by hand, though because they hide down in the inner leaves they are hard to find. Holes in the leaves and little mounds of green droppings are signs that they are about. If you have more than a few plants and not much time, Thuricide or other *Bacillus thuringiensis* preparations are useful. Bt is a bacterium largely specific to butterfly and moth larvae; it paralyzes and then kills the pest.

As with most pests, it's best to treat for them when you have the problem and you can see it's going to be serious. A few stray caterpillars won't hurt a well-developed plant much, but they can ravage a young one. If they are bad in the late summer you can have many stunted winter cabbages.

Cabbage maggots *Hylemya brassicae*

The cabbage maggot is a *real* impediment to the year-round gardener, as the crucifers, which it attacks, represent some of the hardiest and best of the winter crops.

The fall generation of the fly, whose maggots devastate your Chinese cabbages, turnips, and radishes, overwinters as small brown pupae in

the soil not too far from the host
plants. They are usually about three
inches below the surface, but can be
as deep as five or six.

Each pupa hatches out a dark gray
fly, a bit smaller than a house fly, some
time in March or April, depending on
locale and the weather that year. Ac-
cording to Bleasdale et al. (see Appendix D), in England, egg-laying coin-
cides with the blooming of keck, or cow parsley *(Anthriscus sylvestris)*, a
member of the Umbelliferae family and a food source for the adult fly. As
far as I can find out, no one has done studies to see what the flies live
on locally. Dandelion is the only commonly blooming low plant around here
at this time, and it is from a different family. Cherry blossoms, perhaps?
There must be *some* flower, as the flies need to feed before they lay eggs.

For the first day or so after the flies emerge, they are a bit slow and
sit on the soil a lot, but after that you rarely see them unless you catch
them in the act of laying eggs by your plants. After mating, the female
seeks out cauliflowers, broccolis, radishes, and other brassicas and lays
her eggs in the earth by the stems. The eggs hatch into maggots, which
burrow down to the fine root hairs and commence feeding. After about
a month, they pupate and hatch into the midsummer generation of flies.
In most places and seasons, this generation is quite light, and little damage
occurs to June and July transplants. The fall generation, which usually
starts laying right after the mid-August rains in Washington, is heavier,
and a very high percentage of a young crop can be affected.

Maggots sometimes kill plants outright, but just as often they merely
stunt them. Plants will look small but normal to the inexperienced
gardener, but during sunny, dry spells they will suddenly wilt and keel
over. If you then pull up the plants you will find the little white maggots
have almost totally destroyed the roots and stems. The plants have just
been sitting in the soil.

In a wet year some damaged plants will manage to send out new roots
from the stem above the area that has been damaged. However, if your
plants have been too badly set back, they will produce no crop, or at best
a tiny one, and it's best to relegate them to the compost heap and plant
something else. Make sure to destroy any living maggots you find (check
inside the stems, too), as they are the next generation of flies.

The first element of protection against the fly is to ascertain the timing of the generations in your garden. To do this, monitor egg-laying by setting out either cauliflowers or broccolis in early April and leaving a few of them unprotected. Then every day, starting on the second day after planting, carefully brush away the top one-half inch of soil within one to three inches of the stems to look for eggs. If you have transplanted properly—with the first leaves, or cotyledons, below soil level—there will be a lot of stem area above the root zone. The eggs are very small, white, cocoon-shaped things, about one millimeter in length. I simply pinch these out and put them on the path where they will dry out and die. In my experience, the eggs have only been a short distance beneath the soil, so it isn't necessary to disturb the roots when you do this. You can water afterwards with fish or seaweed emulsion if you think your plants need it.

If you start looking just as the flies start laying, you will see only a

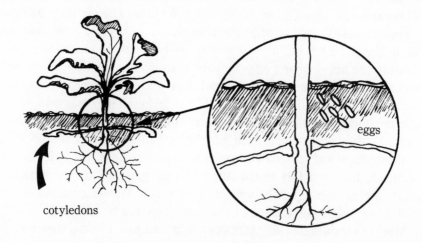

cotyledons

eggs

few eggs at first. In a week or so there may be as many as 12. These higher numbers continue for about a week, and then there is a sudden drop to two or three again. This tells you that the laying is about to stop.

You should keep track of the laying cycle this way for two or three years and make some effort to correlate it to the rest of the environment— early or late, dry or wet season, which plants are in bloom, etc. This will give you an idea of the egg-laying patterns of the flies in your area, and you can *time your main-crop brassica sowings to avoid peak laying.* Probably the very best of the cultural control methods, this allows you to get most of your fall and winter brassicas off and growing with a minimum of damage. Another technique that uses timing is to sow brassicas in September after the last of the August egg-laying and over-winter them under cold frames or, in mild areas, out in rows or beds. There are specific varieties of cabbage for this purpose (see Which Vegetables and Herbs to Grow).

You will still have to protect your early-spring sowings of cabbages, broccolis, turnips, and mustards, and your late-summer sowings of leaf and root brassica crops. To give you some idea of how to do this, I will run through a list of methods people have developed to deal with the cabbage maggot and discuss their feasibility and success—or lack of it! You can choose the ones best suited to your gardening habits and crops.

Placing ashes around transplants and along seedling rows is perhaps the most common barrier method reported by gardeners. What's more, those who use it are convinced it works. My own trials and those at the Washington State University Research Station in Puyallup show that there

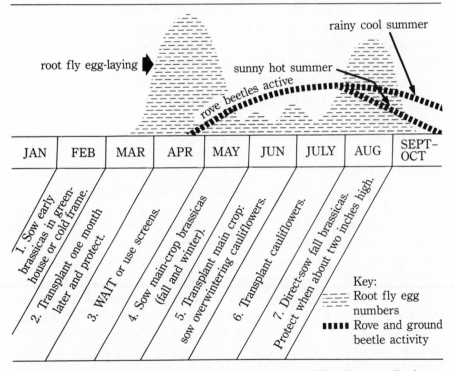

Cabbage Root Fly Egg-Laying Chart

rainy cool summer

root fly egg-laying ▶ sunny hot summer

rove beetles active

| JAN | FEB | MAR | APR | MAY | JUN | JULY | AUG | SEPT–OCT |

1. Sow early brassicas in greenhouse or cold frame.
2. Transplant one month later and protect.
3. WAIT or use screens.
4. Sow main-crop brassicas (fall and winter).
5. Transplant main crop: sow overwintering cauliflowers.
6. Transplant cauliflowers.
7. Direct-sow fall brassicas. Protect when about two inches high.

Key:
- - - Root fly egg numbers
■■■■ Rove and ground beetle activity

Note: The timing for when the fly mates and lays eggs differs from one district to another. You have to check the egg numbers in spring to determine this (see text).

is a *slight* effect against maggots, but that the ashes can corrode the stems of tender transplants. Ashes must also be replaced after rains or irrigation. Once a transplant is established and the stem has toughened up, ashes might be very effective as long as the fly has not already laid eggs by the plant. I have not tried ashes on direct-seeded crops such as turnips and radishes; reports from those who have are varied.

Another popular barrier material is sawdust. Although it may be beneficial as a mulch, I have not found it effective as a barrier to the fly's egg-laying; however, others think it is!

Tar-paper barriers are, I think, plain nonsense. They often blow away, and the holes around the stems of the transplants are almost always large enough to allow the fly to insert her ovipositor right into the soil. In my tests I almost always found as many eggs underneath the collars as in the soil around unprotected plants. A similar technique, developed at the National Vegetable Research Station (NVRS) in England, is to surround the plant with a compressible substance such as foam carpet-underlay. This fits fairly snugly around the stem of the transplants and also acts as a mulch that keeps the root hairs moist and provides a hiding place for predators. These foam collars should be made at least six inches in diameter. The idea here is that the fly, thwarted in her efforts to lay eggs next to the stem, will lay them farther out. In theory, by the time the roots reach the edge of the foam the plants will be big enough to withstand maggot damage.

I tried two kinds of foam collars in the spring of 1982 on broccolis, cauliflowers, and cabbages (about 30 plants in all). While the egg-laying was heavy, I found large numbers of eggs around the stems of the protected plants (as well as around the controls) and under the foam on the surface of the soil. These were easier to remove than the other eggs because I didn't have to hunt through the soil for them. Perhaps they might be easier for the helpful rove and carabid beetles to find, too.

At the very end of the laying period, a large percentage of the eggs apparently hatched out; within two weeks, most of the cauliflowers and some of the broccolis were either dwarfed or dead. Most of the remaining broccolis (which had been good, strong plants 15 inches in height) produced only small heads. I wonder how the National Vegetable Research Station had such good luck with this technique? Maybe it used different foam? Perhaps the cool, clear, dry spring was an important factor. Plant development had been generally retarded, and the fly activity was a good two weeks later than usual in my garden.

Both the Henry Doubleday Research Association and the NVRS report success with the cottage-cheese carton technique. I have not tried this, but apparently it works by creating a dark space around the base of the plant in which the flies will not lay their eggs.

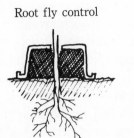

Root fly control

plastic
container

Most of the above techniques are suitable only for transplants and don't work for rows of seeded radishes or turnips. Screened beds are a more suitable solution for these and other seedling brassicas, and even for transplants. Screening works well if there was no immediately previous crop of infested brassicas in the soil. There shouldn't be if you are rotating your crops!

Fly screening from the hardware store, tent netting, cheesecloth (at least 16 threads per inch), Reemay, or muslin all work well. These should be placed over frames, which you can make of wood, wire, or PVC pipe. If you use the caterpillar type of cold frame, you can simply take off the plastic at the right time and replace it with screening. Reemay is light enough to just "float" on the plants. You *must* make sure there are no holes or gaps through which the flies can crawl. I place boards or rocks on the covers all around the edge of the bed and then cover the edges with soil. The plants usually do better under the covers; protected from the wind and getting extra shade, they produce a leafier and more succulent crop.

Tent netting and Reemay have been *my* favorite and most successful barrier controls against cabbage maggots. In 1981 (and following years), my spring mustards were absolutely maggot-free. They grew luxuriantly under the screening in spite of drought. Watering, weeding, and picking them were not problems. The years I have used screening on broccoli, I have had excellent results as long as I was careful to leave no gaps at ground level.

In the area of biological controls, there are several things to try. The first is to encourage the presence of whatever predaceous beetles you happen to have in your environment. Particularly helpful are the Carabidae, or ground beetles, which hide as adults under stones, clods, boards, and other garden debris, and whose soil-dwelling larvae can be recognized by their large pincer jaws. This family includes the European ground beetles: *Calosoma calidum*, a black one with six rows of large copper pits on its wing covers and which gives off a burning acid; and *Calosoma frigidum* and *C. scrutator*, which are black and iridescent, respectively, but have no special common names. Other beneficial beetle families are the Cicindelidae, or tiger beetles, which I have only seen around here in particularly hot summers; and the Staphylinidae, or rove beetles, which are funny little flat guys with cut-off elytra or wing covers. These last are a very large family and can be seen quite early in the year in Northwest gardens. There are good pictures of these in *Rodale's Color Handbook of Garden Insects* (see Appendix D). You should learn to recognize them, as they eat all but the adult stages of this pest. The roves are especially useful in this job, eating many maggots, eggs, and pupae. Unfortunately, like many predators, beetles often emerge later in the season than the fly and thus are better at handling the latter part of the infestations. They are encouraged by ample organic matter, but then so apparently are the flies.

In March when the robins and other ground-feeding birds return, you can dig up the soil in all the areas where you had brassicas the preceding summer, fall, and winter. Leave it like this for a while. The birds will feed on the worms and pupae and any other grubs they can find. If you want to, you can let your chickens into the infested part of the garden. But they will destroy most vegetables and will eat any and every insect they find, good or bad.

A relatively new control to experiment with is the predatory nematode. Though some species of nematodes are harmful in the garden, others parasitize soil larvae, apparently those of the fly family as well as the beetles and moths. So far, all the university tests I've heard about have been done in California, but many gardeners are starting to try them in this area. Some local gardeners have reported good results; others are not as impressed. I tried them on my Chinese cabbage and fall broccoli several times and the results were not fantastic. But at that time I had a fairly heavy clay soil, and apparently the nematodes don't migrate as well in clay and heavy silt loams. It seems that at best the control is a question of percentages. You get fewer maggots and therefore less damage, but you do still get some.

Carrot rust flies   *Psila rosae*

This small fly is a relative of the cabbage root fly and has a similar life cycle. During the early spring (usually April) the adult female lays her eggs in the soil by young carrots. The maggots hatch out and burrow down to the tap root and eat it and the root hairs off. These damaged carrots either don't develop or are stunted.

The maggots pupate through the summer and hatch out in August to go through the process again on the late crops. In some areas, there is an even later hatch in October. Damage from the last two cycles is largely in the form of burrows into the carrot's main root. These have a rusty color that is sometimes hard to see on carrots but stands out on parsnip, celery, and parsley roots, which the maggots also eat.

Strong efforts should be made to control the first generation of flies, as the number of larvae that hatch out will determine the size of the next generation—the one that is so destructive to your winter storage carrots. Some gardeners have reported that raising the alkalinity of the soil with ashes, limestone, or agricultural lime is helpful in protecting the early crops. I can't see exactly why this would deter the maggots. Diatomaceous earth is said to help, too. I haven't done any controlled tests with these materials. If you use them, work them into the rows before sowing.

I've heard that commercial growers in Europe use mosquito netting, cheesecloth, and now Reemay over beds of carrots to prevent the fly from entering.

Sowings after the end of May are usually free of carrot rust flies until the end of August, although you should check this out for your own site. If you time your winter storage carrots to mature before the fall maggots hatch, then lift them and store in a cool, damp situation, you will have next to no damage. The later you harvest carrots in an infested patch, the more damage you will have. You would do well to keep any damaged carrots separate and eat them first.

There is no doubt that carrots overwintered in well-drained soil taste best, though those stored in damp sand are almost as good. Nowadays I lift my winter carrots in October, wash them well, and remove the tops, leaving only a small stub. Then I store them in small or medium-sized cardboard boxes (the ones that are lined with waterproof material are good). These I keep out in the shed. If it goes below 28°F in the shed, I bring them in to a cold room in the house. In deep winter, I always keep the carrot boxes under an old sleeping bag and put a thermometer and a pot of water in with them. If the water freezes more than one-quarter inch deep, I bring the carrots in (water freezes at a higher temperature than biological tissue). If you don't want to dig your carrots all at once, or don't have proper storage facilities, you could try mulching with hay and then covering the mulch with plastic. If you do this right after you have removed the protective screening, you should avoid the egg-laying and later damage. I haven't tried this, but I have seen pictures from the Institute for Biological Husbandry in Switzerland showing this technique being practiced.

In any case, leaving carrots *unprotected* and *undug* only breeds more flies for you to deal with in coming years. Mice and slugs also like carrots and can do quite a bit of damage to the tops through the winter.

Another effective cultural control is to remove the wild umbellifers in your neighborhood. Carrot rust fly larvae eat and overwinter by Queen Anne's lace, hemlock, and wild parsnip. Their eradication can have a considerable effect, as the adult flies do not go much more than a mile from where they hatch to seek hosts. Sad to lose those beautiful Queen Anne's lace flowers, though!

Lettuce root aphids   (*Pemphigus* spp.)

Local entomologists have told me that these are not really a problem in western Washington, but when I have shown slides of these gray, mealy aphids, which attack the roots of lettuce and are only seen when you dig up the plants, gardeners say, "Oh, so that's what that is." So they do trouble some gardens. Late-summer and fall lettuce crops are affected most.

This kind of aphid lives on poplars that grow along rivers and in low, moist areas. During the summer, adult aphids are blown by the wind into your garden. They then burrow into the soil and live around the roots of the lettuces, as well as beets and some other species, weakening the plants. If you have found them to be a serious problem, try the several resistant lettuce varieties that have been developed in Europe. According to Brooks and Halstead, these include Avon Defiance and Avon Crisp.

Slugs   (Gastropoda spp.)

Slugs like cool temperatures and high humidity. They are most active in the fall, when you are trying to get the late plantings of hardy crops up and growing, and in the spring when you're doing the same with the late-spring crops. These are also the times when they lay their little pearl-like eggs under boards, decaying matter, and in garden debris.

Most varieties of slugs are scavengers and scroungers, preferring wilted, dying vegetation and young new stuff. The main reason they devastate your seedlings is that there isn't much else around to eat, especially if you have bare plots of soil with a few tiny plants. There are, unfortunately, a few important exceptions, such as the omnivorous little gray slugs which eat anything, any time. Slugs in general seem to prefer cabbages, pansies, marigolds, and young squash and cucumbers.

I found that slugs abound in greater numbers in the city than in the country. There are so many dark, damp tangles of ivy, clematis, brambles, and garbage-filled trash barrels—slug heaven! Even so, I could keep the predation down to a reasonable level by getting discarded outer cabbage and lettuce leaves at my local grocery and spreading them down the rows or on the edges of the beds. At night I went out with a flashlight and picked up slugs before retiring. Same thing at dawn. During the day the slugs hid under the leaves, so I got them then, too. This helped, but I had to keep at it. An interesting pamphlet from the Henry Doubleday Research Association, *Slugs and the Gardener,* indicates that you could catch slugs in your garden every night for a year and not make a dent in the neighborhood population. These mollusks are migratory, so you would have to organize your whole neighborhood into slug patrols. (Not a bad idea!)

Or you could turn the patrolling over to ducks. Ducks are very fond of slugs. They have a special technique of bill-probing in grass and other vegetation to ferret out low-lying slugs that is very satisfying to watch. Ducks are also friendly, amusing, tasty egg-layers, and they fertilize rather than poison the environment.

In terms of the total picture, ducks don't consume much, if any, nonrenewable energy (none if you let the hens hatch out their own children), and so you are using one more-or-less self-maintaining creature to control another.

If you have a small yard and your ducks show too much of a liking for your garden vegetables, try feeding them greens before you let them in the garden. If this doesn't work, put up a fence and then just use them to patrol the rest of the property, and *you* de-slug the garden itself. The ducks will still be worth it due to that migratory tendency of slugs.

If you have a large country garden and don't like ducks, there is always Deadline (liquid metaldehyde). This can be squirted from a plastic squeeze bottle along hedge borders or around precious plants. Though safer than particulate bait, it can cause serious gastric distress to larger animals that eat it or the slugs poisoned by it, so be cautious. If you have been using metaldehyde or other slug poisons on your property, you are in danger of losing your ducks! Metaldehyde is poisonous to them and will, at the very least, give them a severe stomach ache.

Ducks, of course, are better suited to suburban and rural properties than they are to most city ones, so city dwellers might want to use other forms of control.

Interestingly enough, garter snakes are slug predators, too, though they also consume toads, which are another pest control. The balance is probably in favor of the snakes, so leave them be. Hedgehogs eat slugs, too, but they aren't native to this country. If you are enterprising, maybe you could rent one from a zoo? Chickens don't really seem to relish slugs, but they will scratch up and eat their eggs if you let them into the *fallow* areas of the garden.

One useful technique is to mulch low-lying vegetables such as lettuce with substances slugs don't like to hide under. Wood shavings are good. Hardwoods are best if you can get them. Many gardeners report that barriers of sawdust or wood-shavings in paths and strips around the whole garden help decrease populations in the garden itself. Recent Washington State University research has not demonstrated the effectiveness of this method, though.

Another old trick for slug control is to lay down boards in the garden paths and turn them over every day and stomp on the slugs. I use pansy plants instead of boards; more aesthetic! Slugs love the flowers and hide in great numbers under the plants. I plant pansies in herb beds and other strategic sites around the garden.

The recently developed slug fence seems like a good idea. It's based on the fact that slugs, like rock climbers, have trouble with overhangs.

You can make the fence from flash-
ing, gutters, or any thin sheet metal
you have about. The original design
calls for hardware cloth, but small
slugs can get through the spaces.
Any sort of vegetation leaning
against the fence will serve as a lad-
der, so clean cultivation is the rule.
Unfortunately, the larger your garden, the harder it is to surround it

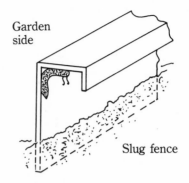

Garden side

Slug fence

with a fence. But these slug fences might be very useful around cold
frames (which unfortunately extend the season for slugs as well as for
plants). Quicklime is very effective around cold frames too, though it must
be renewed after rain and heavy dews. It is good inside propagation boxes,
but should not be used too close to the plants.

I have to admit that I *like* slugs. I think they are beautiful, useful as
scavengers, and have a right to live, especially the native ones. But I need
my garden produce, and I *do* protect my plants when necessary. Having
less time in the last few years, I've resorted to Deadline and to playing
"let's see how far I can toss them." But I feel guilty afterwards.

Flea beetles   *Phyllotreta striolata*

Flea beetles are small, black, striped beetles that leap up like fleas
from tomato, potato, and cabbage plants when you touch or bend over
them. They overwinter in garden trash and weeds and emerge in April
or May to chew little round holes in your seedlings. Their eggs are small
and so are the larvae, which will eat the roots and stems of crops and
weeds. There are one or two generations a year. They are worse in some
soils and gardens than in others.

Some sources say they are more abundant in wet years, but several
years ago, in one of the driest summers in Whatcom County, they devastated both my early and late brassica seedlings. They start on the
cotyledons and then go on to the first true leaves, never giving the plants
a chance.

If your potatoes, tomatoes, and cabbages follow plants that are not hosts
for flea beetles, and the area is large enough to prevent them coming
in from the edges, you will have few problems with them.

I know of no barrier techniques, and I use rotenone. It works well but
needs to be applied once a week at midsummer. Derris and pyrethrum

are said to work, but it's hard to find a source for them. Note that rotenone and pyrethrum also kill worms. In *Grow Your Own Fruit and Vegetables*, L. D. Hills has a good design for a sticky trolly to roll along the rows. The beetles leap up and get stuck.

Diseases

Various forms of rot are hazardous to winter crops. Cultural controls and resistant varieties, when available, are your best defenses.

Root canker attacks parsnips when they grow too big in poorly drained soil during the winter. Canker-resistant varieties are available from Suttons and Chase in England. You can also sow parsnips later, or more thickly, to get smaller roots. Most important of all, use raised beds or other well-drained areas for your root crops.

Cabbages and leeks will get slimy exteriors after damage from frosts. This is not serious if the underlying tissue is healthy.

Lettuces, those fragile beings so important to the salad-minded, are perhaps the most susceptible to rot. Downy mildew (yellow blotches on the leaves) and botrytis, or gray mold (gray fungus and slime around the stem and bottom leaves), are two of the most important. Reports from organic gardeners in Europe say that volcanic ash and finely ground basalt are useful if they're spread on the soil when plants are still in the seedling stage. Powdered garden sulfur has seemed to work the same way for me, but it only reduces the problem; it doesn't eliminate it. In some places where I have gardened, my lettuces were very healthy, so I suspect that soil chemistry or other factors are also involved. It is a good idea to keep lettuce plants well spaced and to make sure the late-summer and fall sowings are in well-drained soil. Cold frames should have constant and adequate ventilation.

Onions are very susceptible to downy mildew on many soils, and the perennial and overwintering types often suffer. Proper spacing in the seedling stage and prompt transplanting are some help. Maybe compost and balanced soil are, too, but the effect of these is more subtle, and I can't judge that yet.

Checking your results

How do you know if your various anti-pest efforts are working? Many people report success with methods that don't work for other gardeners or researchers. Are your strategies really effective, or is the absence of pest or disease due to some other variable like the weather, your compost (or lack of it), or your new sprinkling system?

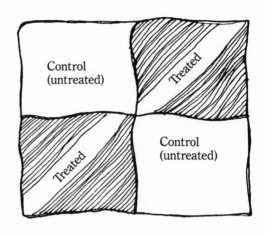

The standard way to test the efficiency of a given method is to use what's known as a Latin square (see the diagram). The new technique is tried out on a block of plants that are growing next to another block of plants, called controls, that are not treated with the new technique. The controls are given the same care in every other respect. There may be blocks like this in several parts of a field, or in several fields, called replicates. The number of replications carried out adds information about the usefulness of a technique. In *Improve Your Garden with Backyard Research*, Lois Levitan offers advice for conducting your own trials (see Appendix D).

Once you've set up your own test plots, compare the treated plants and the controls through the season. If the technique seems to work one year, then you can try it for several more years to rule out climatic variables. Here are three examples to give you some ideas.

A barrier trial for cabbage maggots

In early May of 1978, my first summer in Whatcom County, I did a trial on the effect of sawdust and ashes in preventing maggot damage on cauliflowers. I bought 90 cauliflower plants from a market gardener and laid them out in a long bed as detailed in the chart found on the following page.

This was a rather casual trial. I suppose I should have had several replicates in different parts of the garden, but even growing 90 cauliflowers took rather a lot of energy and space! The first thing to notice is that I was careless and didn't put an even number of plants in each block. That meant I had to do a little extra math to figure out percentages. The second thing to notice is that I had a very high transplant-

failure rate on those blocks with the ashes. This failure was apparent
the day after transplanting; since the stems of the plants were corroded,
I presume it had to do with the caustic effect of the ashes themselves,
which I had piled up around the stems. A similar effect was also noted
at the Western Washington Research Station in Puyallup at their trials,
according to a report in the August 1978 issue of the *Western Washington
Gardener.*

Sawdust Alone	Control (no treatment)	Ashes & Sawdust	Ashes Alone
28 plants 0 transplant failures	19 plants 2 transplant failures	22 plants 5 transplant failures	21 plants 6 transplant failures
8 dead or non-productive by maggot damage.	7 dead or non-productive by maggot damage.	2 dead or non-productive by maggot damage.	1 dead or non-productive by maggot damage.
71% of plants productive.	53% of plants productive.	68% of plants productive.	66% of plants productive.

After this initial transplant loss, though, there weren't as many losses
from maggot activity in the ash and sawdust/ash groups as there were
in the sawdust-alone and control groups. I'm not exactly sure how to in-
terpret this data, but there are several possibilities. I think the experiment should be redesigned and run again. For one thing, when I started
checking egg-laying on the second day after transplanting, I didn't find
many eggs. As it turned out later, that was about the time that egg-laying
drops off in this locale. The peak is usually in April.

If I *were* to redesign this experiment, I would make earlier as well as
later sowings. I would surround the stems of some of the transplants
with paper to protect them from the ashes, wrapped tightly enough to
prevent the fly from crawling down it to lay her eggs. As soon as the
stems were hardened, I would remove the paper and pile up the ashes.
(That is quite a bit of extra work, of course, which is one reason I've
settled instead on using netting. I figure one procedure that protects a
lot of plants at once is less work than fiddling with many plants many
times.)

A slug-repellent trial

This experiment was sent in by a Seattle Tilth member some years
ago. I quote from his letter. The herb-based substance he was using was

Fertosan Slug Destroyer, sold in Wales and England to repel slugs and prevent them from breeding. You can purchase it from the Henry Double-day Research Association (see Appendix C), but they say that gardeners have reported mixed results. The company will not release any information about it, and it isn't registered for use in the United States. When I need something of that sort I now use liquid metaldehyde. I guess I prefer to use a low-grade *known* poison to an unknown compound.

Dear Binda,

Well, I'm finally getting around to sending you a letter about my results with Fertosan Slug Destroyer. I have been waiting for the appearance of more slugs (our hard winter seemed to have really done them in this year) so I would have definitive results. The results are good.

My most recent test was to set out two saucers of beer (slugs love it) about five feet apart near my compost pile. Around one of the saucers I put Fertosan as directed, to a radius of about a foot and a half. The next day there were about a half-dozen slugs in the unprotected saucer and none in the protected saucer.

I got similar results in my potato patch. The spuds usually have quite a problem with the [small gray] slugs. With the use of Fertosan there were none of these pests in the plants, though I did find them in near-by unprotected plants. The protection did seem to wear off after about two months.

In general, I would say that the material works very well. I would, however, like some further assurance that the material is safe; it is, after all, a chemical.

Sincerely,
R. Aaron Falk

Actually, I believe that Mr. Falk is mistaken, and that Fertosan is most likely mainly herbs, perhaps tansy and other noxious European weeds, rather than "chemicals" in the industrial sense. However, the question is a bit moot as Fertosan is so hard to get in this country—which throws you on your own initiative again. So get out there and gather some of our own noxious herbs, grind them into a powder, and see if you can design your own experiment to see if they are good slug deterrents! Remember, though: poisons are poisons, whether chemical or "natural," so avoid poison hemlock and the like.

Companion planting

This third example of an experiment to check out gardening theories is from the Henry Doubleday Research Association newsletters. The HDRA is a membership organization for the purpose (among others) of researching improved methods of organic gardening and farming. Each year its winter newsletter lists experiments that members can undertake. You write in and get directions, seed or whatever else is required. In the fall, you report on your results. HDRA has members and local chapters all over, so the organization gets quite a lot of information this way. It also does experiments on its trial grounds in Coventry, England. In 1978 the HRDA commenced a series of trials to test the companionship effect of certain vegetables and herbs on each other, as reported by Philbrick and Gregg in *Companion Plants* (see Appendix D) and repeated ad nauseam by gardening advisors and authors.

To begin with, the HDRA decided against using the Latin square common in experimental plots of fertilizer or varietal trials. Instead they planted a circular bed to work out the best distances between rows for new varieties. The idea here is that in the middle of the circle the two complementary (or uncomplementary) crops would be closest and have the greatest effect on each other, and at the perimeter they would be farthest apart and have the least effect. One HDRA newsletter reported on a trial of peas and garlic, a combination said by Philbrick and Gregg to be inhibiting to the peas. Later newsletters carried reports on trials with other combinations of vegetables, and some with herbs that were said to repel insects. They also reported on work done by research scientists in Australia and the U.S. They tried out parallel rows of supposedly complementary crops such as beets and onions, cabbages and dill, etc.

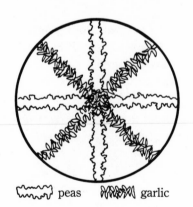

〰〰 peas   〰〰 garlic

Circle bed for testing the effect of increasing distance between two different vegetables.

In none of these reports by the HDRA or others were any of the effects (yields, insect infestations, etc.) numerically significant. The only exception was interplantings of vegetables with the herb wormwood (a species of *Artemesia*), one of the known and accepted allelopathic plants. Allelopathic plants have a negative effect, usually through root secretions, on many other plants in the vicinity. This effect can be worse in nutrient-deficient soil.

My reaction to these reports is to guess that Philbrick and Gregg's original findings were idiosyncratic and that authors who repeat their information (without thorough trials), in books or other ways, are capitalizing on ill-founded information.

I'm not one to demand that everything be proven by "science"—quite the opposite. It's just that I'm bored when people endlessly repeat what plants "like" other plants without even crediting Philbrick and Gregg, who themselves requested feedback from other gardeners on their experiences. Further, following those lists slavishly, instead of making your own experiments and observations in your own locale, is contrary, I feel, to the practice of good gardening. Or good living.

What's more, my feeling about our common vegetables is that, since they are mostly derived from weeds that have associated with people and their manure heaps for thousands of years, they are by nature fairly flexible in their associations and, rather like city folk, can live cheek by jowl with their neighbors and not suffer unduly.

This is not to say, of course, that in their wild state they didn't form natural associations of mutual benefit; undoubtedly they did. But your garden and the varieties you sow are not terribly close to the "wild" state. Having said that, I will add that there are many ways in which plants are known to be useful to each other, and that horticulturalists have been utilizing this in their gardens for years. Some of the earliest were the native Americans who grew beans up their cornstalks in some areas (this is still practiced in such places as Mexico). But this doesn't work in all climates. I haven't found it useful here, for instance, due to our cooler climate.

Many studies have been done by plant ecologists and agronomists on the varying effects of plants on each other. An excellent compilation of those relevant to your garden is available in Robert Kourik's book, *Designing and Maintaining Your Edible Landscape.* Another source is the Agroecology Program at UC Santa Cruz, as often reported in their newsletter, *The Cultivar* (see Appendix D). Just remember when you read about well-done studies demonstrating effects between various crops that many of these are done in *fields,* many are done in climates different from your own, and many may be done with varieties other than the ones you choose to use. In other words, watch for the variables, and don't take much for granted.

> *Nothing exists but momentarily in its present form and color. One thing flows into another and cannot be grasped. Before the rain stops we hear a bird. Even under the heavy snow we see snowdrops and some new growth.*
>
> —Suzuki Roshi

WHICH VEGETABLES AND HERBS TO GROW

Introduction

I've tried to make the vegetable list as comprehensive as possible so that you will be exposed to the full range of vegetables suitable for cool-season cropping. I don't suggest you grow all or even most of them in your first years. There are many I haven't grown myself; information on these vegetables comes from others or from books.

In most instances, I don't give general cultural requirements unless they are not available elsewhere. Not only am I trying to keep this book short, but I think that you'll benefit from reading *many* gardening books, especially the better ones. No one book says it all. Once you realize there is no single "right" way to make a garden, then you are freer to experiment on your own.

Using this guide

The vegetables are arranged in four sections. First are the members of the Cruciferae family—the important brassicas, including cabbage, kale, broccoli, and so on. Next come onions and other vegetables that will survive and even thrive over the maritime Northwest winter. The final group includes herbs suitable for winter cropping. The entries in each section are listed alphabetically; if you're not sure where to look for a particular species, please refer to the index.

Terms

"Sow" refers to putting seed in the ground (or pot, plug flat, etc.). The term "plant" refers to putting a plant in the ground (transplanting).

I experienced difficulty finding Latin names for some varieties, as many garden books and seed catalogs don't routinely list them (even those that do sometimes disagree, as taxonomists regularly update nomenclature). I did the best I could, though there are probably a few errors.

Taxonomy comes from:

Bailey, Liberty Hyde, and Ethel Zoe Bailey; revised by the staff of L.H. Bailey Hortorium. *Hortus Third: A Concise Dictionary of Plants Cultivated in the United States and Canada.* New York: Macmillan Publishing Co., Inc., 1976.

Richard Fitter, Alastair Fitter, and Marjorie Blamey. *The Wild Flowers of Britain and Northern Europe.* New York: Scribner & Sons, 1974.

S.G. Harrison, G.B. Masefield, and Michael Wallis. *Oxford Book of Food Plants.* London: Oxford University Press, 1973.

Lawrence D. Hills. *Grow Your Own Fruit and Vegetables.* London: Faber and Faber, 1975.

C. Leo Hitchcock and Arthur Cronquist. *Flora of the Pacific Northwest.* Seattle: University of Washington Press, 1973.

Tsang & Ma. *The Tsang & Ma International Catalog.* Belmont: Tsang & Ma, 1979.

Hardiness

I have designated each vegetable as very hardy, hardy, or half-hardy. *Very hardy* plants include leeks, kale, salsify, and corn salad, which may live through temperatures as low as 0°F. *Hardy* plants such as cabbages and onions will usually survive frosts of 10°F. *Half-hardy* plants die at freezing or a little below (18°F at the most). These designations are for the purposes of this book only; most of the plants mentioned are hardy compared to other garden vegetables. All freeze-out data are from maximum/minimum thermometers in my own and other gardens in the northwestern part of Washington State. Remember that these numbers are approximate. A temperature of 10°F will cause greater damage if it lasts for three days than if it lasts for three hours. Several hard freezes during the winter will cause greater damage to your plants than one. A strong wind along with a low temperature will cause even greater damage. If it snows and then plunges to 10°F, you will get less damage to the covered plants than if it freezes to the same degree without snow cover.

Sowing dates

When discussing the time to sow certain varieties I often say something like "June in the north, July in the south." By north I am referring to northern Washington and southern British Columbia; by south, mid-Oregon. There is about a month's difference in sowing and planting dates between these two locations, which are approximately 300 miles apart. You will have to adjust these dates for your particular site. If you live outside the maritime Northwest, see Appendix A, Gardening Outside the Maritime Northwest.

Seed sources

Where a variety is not well known or is available from only one or two seed companies, I have included the appropriate seed company abbreviation in the listing. Sources are not given for varieties presently carried by three or more companies. Remember that, since seed companies shift inventory like any other business, their offerings may change over the years. See Seed Companies in Appendix C for addresses.

ABL	Abundant Life Seed Foundation
BARB	John Barber Ltd.
BLUM	Seeds Blüm
BURP	W. Atlee Burpee Co.
CCS	Chase Compost Seeds
COOK	The Cook's Garden
DAM	William Dam Seeds Ltd.

HAST	Hastings
JSS	Johnny's Selected Seeds
NICH	Nichols Garden Nursery
PARK	G. W. Park Seed Co.
RED	Redwood City Seed Co.
RICH	Richters
SSE	Seed Savers Exchange
STK	Stokes Seed Company
SUF	Suffolk Herbs
SUT	Suttons Seeds Ltd.
TER	Territorial Seed Co.
TILL	Tillinghast Seed Co.
TSA	Tsang & Ma
WELL	Well-Sweep Herb Farm

Varieties

Many garden books don't even list varieties because they change so rapidly. The authors feel there is no point in recommending varieties that may be gone from the market in another 10 years.

I have broken with this convention for several reasons. First, it helps gardeners distinguish between summer and cool-season versions of the same vegetable. Second, many breeders are switching over to producing hybrids and therefore so are wholesalers and retailers. If you know the names of the best open-pollinated winter varieties, it will help you recognize them in catalogs, especially in the *Garden Seed Inventory* published by the Seed Savers Exchange, a group of people who save older varieties. If you purchase these varieties now, you have some chance of getting to know them and learning how to save seed before they disappear from the market. Although hybrids are not necessarily bad per se (in fact, a few are very superior), they are usually tightly controlled by the company that produces them and therefore expensive. Third, the name of an old variety can give clues to the nature of present or future ones. If you read in a catalog that a certain cabbage, carrot, or kale, hybrid or open-pollinated, has been developed from one you know, you will have some idea of how this new one might perform in your garden.

My last and perhaps main reason for listing winter varieties was that I hoped to make the process of choosing winter garden crops a little easier for you than it was for me. I've spent 15 years poring over catalogs and trying out vegetables in my garden. Sometimes it was a bore to grow 22 kinds of cabbages and seven varieties of leeks all in one year, but it sure taught me a lot. The least I can do is pass on my impressions to you. And impressions is just what they are. At no time have I had the capital or time available to carry out the intensive varietal trials that a funded research station or a seed company can do. Thus, my choices are often idiosyncratic and based on the soil in my garden, the local climate, my taste buds, and how much attention I was paying to the matter each year while tending to my family and business.

Unfortunately, in the last few years the seed business has changed dramatically, and many of the old European varieties that work so well in the maritime Northwest are being dropped. Also, the quality of the seed stock of those that have been kept is dropping due to lack of breeder attention, improper roguing, and other factors. Briefly, companies stand to make far more money from hybrids that they themselves have developed and patented than they do from open-pollinated varieties, which any grower can produce at will.

If you are a beginner, it will help you to begin by trying some of the recommended varieties—though if you are reading this book 10 years from now, you may find that catalogs offer entirely different stock. The important thing is to find the *equivalent* variety for the job, whether it's an overwintering cabbage or a good cold-frame lettuce. And the second important thing is to become a seed saver. Choose some of the old varieties that do well in your garden and help save them. Join the Seed Savers Exchange and trade seeds.

Since we probably can't save everything, we should concentrate on whatever we can do best in each of our areas. In the maritime Northwest, our biennials should take high priority. Among these are the cabbages (the fall and winter greens, reds, and the savoys), the late Brussels sprouts, the overwintering cauliflowers, and the leeks. Annuals such as the Asian cruciferous greens and the winter lettuces can best be selected in winter areas that present a challenge to the varieties but don't kill them outright. If seed savers in any given area coordinate, they can parcel out endangered varieties to adopt and save. (The Seed Savers Exchange considers a variety endangered when only one company is carrying it.)

Also, get to know the people at seed companies in your area that are involved in this process. In short, do what our ancestors had to do in order to have vegetables on their tables. It's already very late, so if you want to have a choice of varieties, get to work!

Crucifers

The Cruciferae family is so large and important to the year-round gardener that it merits its own section. Included in the group are *Brassica oleracea* (cabbages, broccolis, cauliflowers, Brussels sprouts, and some kales), *B. pekinensis (Pe-Tsai,* Napa, Chihili), the closely related radishes *(Raphanus sativus),* horseradish *(Armoracia rusticana),* watercress *(Nasturtium officinale),* and American winter cress *(Barbarea verna).*

These species form a horticultural group with similar needs, pests, and diseases. When you practice crop rotation, they should, with a few exceptions, be considered as a group and *rotated together.*

The exceptions are watercress (which belongs in water or moist soil), horseradish and winter cress (which can go in permanent herb beds), and rocket (which is best grown as a catch crop).

Since our most important brassicas evolved in northwest Europe's maritime climate, they adapt well to *our* maritime climate and have special pertinence to this region.

Most of the European brassicas are heavy nitrogen feeders, do well with lime, and are susceptible to attack by clubroot, cabbage loopers, imported cabbageworms, cabbage maggots, and gray aphids. These brassicas usually benefit from transplanting, as it aids their root system. For individual preferences and cultural tips, see the books by Hills, Simons, and Shewell-Cooper listed in Appendix D.

The Asian brassicas are a little harder to work with, because their sensitivity to daylength makes it necessary to plan their planting times carefully. It's also harder to find cultural information on them. But they are delicious and extremely useful for cold-frame work in more severe climates. Hills, Simons, Solomon, Chan, and Larkcom have some cultural suggestions, as do the catalogs from Tsang & Ma, Johnny's Selected Seeds, and Territorial. Rodale Press has put out a good pamphlet, *Summary of Cool Weather Crops for Solar Structures,* that discusses the use of frames and includes seed sources and recipes.

Note that the crucifers, the *B. napus* types, contain goitrogenic substances (they lower the activity of your thyroid, the thermostat of your body), so I'd go slow on them if I were you, or eat seaweed to balance it out. On the other hand, crucifers are now also believed to play an important role in the prevention of cancer.

Broccoli   *Brassica oleracea italica*

Broccoli is one of America's favorite vegetables, and in milder areas such as Seattle it can be harvested almost year-round. Gardeners in colder sites will have to do without from early winter until spring. There are good varieties for each season, and you would do well to use each when it grows best.

Broccolis come in green, white, and purple (which turns green when cooked). Their leaf shape and resprouting ability are their distinguishing characteristics. In England, winter cauliflowers were popularly called broccoli, kale was known as borecole, and what we usually buy as broccoli in the store was known as Calabrese after the Calabrian region of Italy, where those varieties originated. This, of course, led to a certain amount of confusion in nomenclature, and seed catalogs on different sides of the Atlantic would list the same variety under different headings. Since the establishment of variety legislation by the European Economic Community (EEC), though, this seems to have been straightened out. Cauliflowers are sold as such, and broccoli usually includes Calabrese types as well as the overwintering sprouting broccolis of both colors.

Summer and fall varieties   Hardy

Italian Green Sprouting
DeCicco
Waltham
Various hybrids

These belong to the Calabrese type we are all familiar with. In very mild locations such as Seattle they can be grown through the late fall and winter from July and August sowings. Temperatures much below 18°F do them in, and their heads are very susceptible to rot from rain. In colder districts you can have them until early December if the fall and winter are mild, but they need to be sown by June. You can also sow in late January or early February in heated frames for an early spring crop. Some of the new commercial varieties have excellent hardiness.

Overwintering varieties   Very hardy

Purple Sprouting
White Sprouting (SUT, TER)
Nine Star Perennial (SUT, BARB)

These are sown in late May in the north, later in the south, and overwinter in the immature state to form heads in early spring. The Purple Sprouting types are the best, to my mind, but some whites are all right.

They are very hardy and have survived 6°F in my garden, withstanding northeasters with much gallantry. They are *large* plants, taking up a good 30 inches each way, especially in March when they start to produce their small purple or white heads. The heads keep coming for a month or so but get progressively smaller as time goes on. By the time they get as thin as asparagus, the little florets are wonderful in salads. After that, you can turn them under.

The main problem, other than size, with overwintering broccolis' is that it harbors the gray aphid, which will then have ready access to your young spring transplants. The chance of these colonies overwintering is reduced if you spray the plants in the fall or early spring (see Sharecroppers).

I have not kept Nine Star Perennial over to see if it really lasts several years as the catalogs say. I don't know if it would be worth it, as it would interfere with crop rotation and general garden organization. And, of course, it would harbor pests such as the cabbage aphid.

Brussels sprouts *B. oleracea gemmifera*

Brussels sprouts, along with kale, parsnips, and leeks, are the epitome of winter-hardy vegetables. They are available from September till March. In April you can eat the sprouts as they start to flower; they taste much like broccoli then and are good in stir-fries and salads. In fact, I think Brussels sprouts are better sautéed than steamed. They are also excellent in soups.

Early varieties   Half-hardy

If you like to have a continuous supply of Brussels sprouts from September on, you can start off the season with some of the American types, such as Jade Cross, Long Island, and Catskill, or Early Dwarf Danish. Personally, I don't want to bother with picking sprouts in the early fall when there is such an abundance of cabbage. Also, for some reason I haven't been able to get many of these types to form well for me. The sprouts grow loose heads and, since they are close to the ground and jam-packed together, maggots can come up from the root system in wet falls and tunnel into them. Their tight spacing also makes the sprouts vulnerable to rot, and they are not *really* hardy. Two more reasons not to grow them for the winter.

Midseason and late varieties Very hardy

Stiekema (DAM)
Cambridge series
Bedford series (SUT)
Roodnerf series (TER, SUT)
Rubine (COOK, DAM)
Various new hybrids

A great deal of breeding work has been done lately with Brussels sprouts, and it is getting harder to find the open-pollinated varieties. The above list includes good series that have midseason and late types within them. They grow medium to tall in height: 24 to 42 inches. This allows the sprouts to be well spaced along the stems and helps prevent rot. The sprouts are generally small and very tight. The English varieties, Cambridge and Bedford, tend to have bigger, elongated sprouts with more of that disagreeable, hot, "cabbagey" taste.

I have been happiest with the Dutch-bred Roodnerfs. They are medium-tall and less inclined to lean over in the wind than the real giants. They have good-sized, hard, round sprouts with a very sweet flavor. The Roodnerfs also seem more tolerant of poor growing conditions. Stiekema and Roodnerf Early Button are excellent midseason types; Roodnerf Rido and Late Supreme are good late ones. Rido is shorter and so perhaps better-suited to windy areas. As of this writing, Suttons is still carrying Roodnerf Early Button, and Territorial continues to sell the Late Supreme. I think that experienced gardeners would do well to attempt saving seed of the other two varieties if they have the room and the inclination, since Brussels sprouts respond strongly to environmental influences.

Brussels sprouts. . . show very wide variation that is caused partly by the environment and partly by genetic differences. This renders selection difficult, and in the past quite numerous commercial strains have failed to meet the requirements of all growers. As a consequence this crop, more than other cole crops, has been subjected to extensive selection by the growers themselves. The resulting growers' strains are sometimes adapted to the growing conditions in a certain locality. For instance, types selected on a heavy soil may show rank growth and produce loose sprouts when grown on light soils, and strains from a light soil may remain too short-stemmed on a heavy soil.

Variety trials have shown that there are also strains that can be satisfactorily grown almost anywhere, and these are attractive to the trade.

—M. Nieuwhof, *Cole Crops,* 1969, p. 79.

Cabbage *B. oleracea capitata*

It is possible to harvest cabbage most of the year if you match varieties with planting dates. Whether you want to eat that much cabbage is another question! I lose interest in them during the summer when there is so much else. But they are useful, very easy to grow, and taste so much better from the garden.

Early spring varieties   Hardy

These are quick little cabbages, often with pointed heads, that are sown in September and early October and *overwintered* in cold frames until

Spring
cabbage

they can be planted out in February or March. In some very mild districts, you can overwinter them outside. They tend to be loose and often bolt before they form much of a head, but they are tender, and because April to June is a period rather bereft of greens, I find them worth the effort. Jersey Wakefield, April, Express, Greyhound, and First Early Market are good varieties currently available in

American catalogs. If you do well with these, try others from the English catalogs.

One of the best things about these autumn-sown types is that they are too big and well established to be much affected by cabbage maggots in the spring—a great bonus!

Green cabbages for standing and storage   Very hardy

I sow these, and the savoys and the reds, in plugs from late April to early May (later in the south) for main-crop cabbages. I used to use a seed bed because it was easier to keep them together for watering, feeding, and weeding. But plugs in flats are even easier, and the risk of transplanting shock is far less in the hot days of late June and early July. The trick is to use a plug that is big enough that the young brassica won't be crowded at the end of the four to six weeks it needs to become big enough to plant out. Crowding young brassicas causes *stopping*; they become dwarfed, reddish around the edges of the leaves, and look gray-green and tough instead of a lovely succulent green as they should (unless, of course, they are red cabbages, but you know what I mean). It's a waste of time to set stopped brassicas out, and don't ever waste your money buying them. It's very common to see them in this state at supermarket nurseries.

I also sow Brussels sprouts, late broccoli, fall purple cauliflower, kale, and Purple Sprouting broccoli in these plugs. I sow the overwintering cauliflowers a month later.

A month after sowing, I choose the best plants and put them out in their permanent beds. If you are using the seed-bed method, soak the seedlings well the day before and then do your transplanting on a gray, misty day; if the weather doesn't oblige, transplant at night and keep a fine spray on the seedlings during the hottest hours. The idea is not so much to make water available to their roots (which you're doing anyhow) but to keep the atmosphere around their leaves cool and moist. This way they are growing again in a couple of days.

The heads are ready to eat by September or October but will stand in the garden until March in more or less good condition depending on weather and variety. I always leave the better-looking ones for last.

As I live in northeaster territory, I also pull a few cabbages out by their roots and store them in a box or a heap in damp wood shavings or sawdust. They keep fine this way in a shed, and even if they freeze somewhat, they'll thaw out with little or no damage. I also use them to make low-salt kraut and *kim chee* in gallon jars and store the pickles in the refrigerator when the cabbage has finished fermenting.

I used to have many non-hybrid favorites among the winter cabbages, but their seed is hard to get now due to EEC variety regulations. Some of these were Glory of Enkhuizen, Christmas Drumhead, and the Langedijker series. So you'll have to try the rather expensive hybrids (admittedly often very good), search among the more conservative catalogs, or try the Seed Savers Exchange. The Henry Doubleday Research Association has a varietal seed bank, and it may have good old winter varieties. The very best varieties, though, were the Dutch rather than the English ones.

Red cabbages   Very hardy

Meteor, Mammoth Red Rock, the red storage cabbages (STK), and the Langedijker Winterkeepers (DAM) are all good fall and winter sorts. I haven't noticed much difference between these last varieties in terms of their ability (very good) to withstand rain, rot, and freezes.

Savoy cabbages   Very hardy

Savoy cabbages are not well known in America, but I enjoy them more and more each year. They are loose, open cabbages and don't have a very

long shelf life, which probably contributes to their lack of popularity. But they taste wonderful, have greener inner leaves than other cabbages, and are certainly worthy of attention by the winter gardener and cook. They are also very beautiful. The old varieties are the hardiest of the cabbages and stand well in the rain and snow.

Their name comes from an area in southeast France and is also used as an adjective to describe the intense crinkling of their leaves. This is thought to impart some extra hardiness to plants that have it (for instance, Cold Resistant Savoy spinach).

I find Chieftain to be an early sort and not really hardy where I garden. There have been attempts in the trade to breed savoys that store well, but I feel these are best ignored by the home gardener.

My favorite early savoys were Kappertjes, which are small, very early ones for eating in September and October, and Ormskirk (SUT), a standard English type that comes in autumn and winter forms. Ormskirk is super-hardy and stands until March, or later in a wet, cold spring.

January King is an old standard, a well-deserved favorite, and now one of the few open-pollinated winter cabbages left. Before the EEC rulings, it was just as often listed with the green cabbages, but now it has been settled as a savoy. It has beautiful red tinges, and it's tough! (It stands the weather *and* takes longer cooking to soften up.) January King is also really delicious. It has several hybrid descendants.

Cauliflower   *B. oleracea botrytis*

Growing summer cauliflower has always been an arduous undertaking for me, but fall and overwintering ones are easier and rewarding. I treat them like cabbages, sowing the fall cauliflowers with the main-crop cabbages and the overwintering ones a month later in June. I transplant them after a month and keep them good and moist until they start growing again.

If you are a beginning gardener, you might want to avoid cauliflowers in the first year and devote your space to a more productive and reliable crop. Cauliflowers are low in Vitamin A in comparison with other crucifers (though fair in other nutrients) and the winter varieties take up lots of space—three feet each way. If you do decide to grow them, make sure that any manures you add are well composted, that you keep the plants well watered in dry spells, and that you transplant them before they get crowded. Hills, Shewell-Cooper, and Seymour have interesting sections on cauliflowers in their books.

Fall varieties   Hardy

These include such types as Purple Sicilian (ABL) and Autumn Veitch. They are sown with the main-crop cabbages and later transplanted at the same time. They are ready to eat by September and usually done by late November, depending on your locale. In a *very* mild location, a slightly later sowing will give plants that crop on into December (I harvested Veitch Autumn Giant in January in my Seattle garden), and in English catalogs you could find varieties specifically for this time. I currently garden so far north that I don't experiment with them. (That doesn't mean *you* shouldn't!)

The older open-pollinated fall cauliflower varieties are also slipping away from us, though maybe not as fast as the cabbages. Stokes, Territorial, and Abundant Life have some at this writing.

Overwintering types   Very hardy

These are sown very late. I sow overwintering varieties in June, but the British Columbia research station starts them later and so do the farmers in the Skagit Valley—must be something peculiar about my site or soil! If you want to try them, make some successive sowings through the summer to see what the best dates for you are. If I sow them much later than June and transplant in July, they are not only hit by drought, but also devastated by cabbage maggots. Commercial growers usually direct-sow and use insecticides and don't have to worry about this.

There are many varieties of these overwintering cauliflowers: the English Winters, the very fine Walcherins, the Armado series, and others. Unfortunately, they are not all available in American catalogs, and even British retail seed catalogs can't match the excellent selection that is available to the wholesale trade. Still, even with those available (SUT, TER, ABL), you can have fine crops from late February till June.

If you have a large family, you will want to put overwintering cauliflowers on 36-inch centers in beds; if you have a small family, try 24 inches, or else you won't be able to eat the monsters at one meal. In a good year, the late April/early May ones are 18 inches across—and if you have even two or three of those ripening at once, you've got to trade or give them away. By June they are overwhelming. Planting at later dates also reduces the final size.

Chinese cabbage   *B. pekinensis cylindrica*   Hardy

All fall types

Chinese cabbage, the big heading sort, responds best to decreasing daylength and temperatures. That makes it a good fall crop and, in mild locales, a winter one. But it's not so good for spring. I use one non-heading type and the bok choy types *(B. chinensis)* for late winter and early spring cold-frame work (see Mustard section). I have had some Chinese cabbages last through January, when they start to flower. The flowers are great in salads.

The Chinese store their mature cylindrical cabbages through the winter in unheated cold frames made of mud bricks, or in pits covered with mats. This keeps them blanched and in good condition.

Since they are sown in late summer, the plants are seriously bothered by the cabbage maggot, and it pays to make an effort to protect them one way or another. An extra-early sowing made in late June or early July is well on its way before the mid-August maggot attacks. Unfortunately, in hot summers these sowings have a tendency to bolt, so take extra care to grow them in fertile soil with good irrigation. These later crops can be covered with screening or mulched with sawdust.

Collards *B. oleracea acephala* Very hardy

Vates/Champion
Georgia (HAST, BLUM)   Cabbage Collards (HAST)

These small, open cabbages, very popular in the southern U.S. and in black communities, are useful greens in the late winter. They were known as coleworts in England. I suspect they were brought over by the Scots immigrants to Appalachia and selected to survive in the South. There are very interesting varieties from Portugal and Italy, too. Collards can be thought of as transitional varieties between the curly-leaved kales and the "primitive" wild cabbage of Europe. They are naturally hardy, with much variation, and if you grow 20 or so plants of a not overly selected strain, you will see this diversity.

Breeders in the Southeast, where collards are a winter staple, have worked with them more than anyone else. They are grown commercially over much of the Piedmont area, and though often not harvestable in the depths of winter, they are good late-fall and early-spring crops. In the Northwest, a mid-July sowing will produce a good crop. They will go down to at least 15°F, and in most Northwest winters can be harvested continuously, like kale. They have a similar high vitamin content.

Cress

Barbarea verna Very hardy
    American Winter Cress (common weed, RICH)
Lepidium sativum Half-hardy
    Garden Cress (RICH, STK, ABL)

You will often find *Barbarea verna* (known as American winter cress or upland cress) growing wild. In fact, it thoroughly naturalized itself in my old Seattle garden, where I started it from seed one fall and then ignored it because I found I didn't like it much. It tastes like a hot watercress. A small, innocuous plant, it would do well in the herb garden, where you could just let it be and gather small amounts for winter salads.

Lepidium sativum, the other cress, is more succulent and is often grown as sprouts (as well as in the garden) in Europe. Hills has a good description of how to do this under a cardboard box. In Europe cress is grown for the market in little plastic trays. Customers take it home, put it on the windowsill or in the fridge, and snip off sections for their salads.

Kale   *B. oleracea acephala* and *B. napus pabularia*   Very hardy

Kales, along with leeks, turnips, parsnips, and the hardiest cabbages, formed the mainstay of later-winter vegetable eating for Northern Europeans for many centuries. Gardens in Scotland were known as "kailyards" (since Scotland runs from about 56°N to 59°N, this has interesting implications for coastal Alaskans).

Tall
curled kale

There are many varieties of kale that I have read about but not seen listed in catalogs: old standards of self-sufficient gardeners and farmers that have disappeared along with so many other varieties since the Industrial Revolution, with its freezers, trucking, and changes in eating patterns. But kale, though you might not find it in the supermarkets, is high in vitamins A, C, E, and K. Being so hardy, it merits your attention, if not midwinter devotion, and a place in your garden. The spring sprouts, tender and broccoli-like, are superb. And the flowering kales, as well as being highly ornamental, are quite palatable.

There are two forms of kale. The first stems from *B. oleracea* and includes dwarf and tall Scotch, semi-dwarf and tall curled, cottager's, and thousand-head. Thousand-head is huge and used for stock. Cottager's is pretty big, too, with lots of red tints to it. It is very hardy and has gone down to 4°F in my garden with no damage. I don't think much of the taste, but it's good for the chickens if you live in the mountains. The others (which are very similar except in height) can be started in May or June in flats or in the cabbage seed bed. They can then be set out at their normal spacing (24 inches between plants) a month later. There are F1 hybrids of curled kale around today, but I don't see any reason to go that route, especially since it's so easy to save kale seed (just make sure there aren't any other *B. oleracea* relatives flowering at the same time).

The other kinds of kale do not transplant well. They stem from *B. napus pabularia* and include Siberian, Ragged Jack, Russian (ABL), Hanover, and asparagus kale. These forms are related to the rapes and rutabagas (they have a different number of chromosomes than the *B. oleracea* types) and include some of the superior salad kales.

Russian kale

These types can be sown directly in July or August on 18-inch centers. If you are worried about germination, sow a few extra seeds and then thin (feed thinnings to the livestock in September or eat them yourself). Unless your soil is awful, don't manure or fertilize before you sow; the plants will grow too fast and won't be as hardy.

I usually have three to six plants of the tall curly kale, and two to three of the Siberian, which feeds a two-person family and from five to seven chickens that have partial free range. I use the curled through March, when it starts to flower and I've cut all the sprouts of any size. Then I pull it up, turn in the soil, and turn my attention to the Siberian. It will last approximately another month in a cool spring. The flowers of these or any other brassica are delicious in salads, so I usually leave one plant of some type somewhere in the garden. More often than not, it's the one I'm saving for seed that year.

I like dwarf Siberian for eating raw, especially in spring when the new sprouts and leaves are very tender. Some folks I know eat Scotch and the green curled varieties raw too, but I find them tough and strong-flavored (except in the spring), even though they do improve after a few frosts. I prefer them in soups and stews, where they are delicious. Russian, like Siberian, is a tender, very attractive kale, striking in salads at all times of the year. But it is not terribly hardy and will die out around 25°F. Its best quality is that you can start it all through the summer and it won't bolt on you or turn bitter (except perhaps in a very hot July or August).

Kohlrabi *B. oleracea caulorapa*   Half-hardy

Purple Vienna
Vienna

Kohlrabi, or Hungarian turnip as it is sometimes called, is mainly a summer crop. But if you like it, you can sow as early as the beginning of March under frames and a little later outside. For the fall crop, sow during the end of July and the first bit of August.

The Europeans are always churning out new, less woody versions of kohlrabi, so it won't do to recommend any here — they will just be different next year, like new cars. If you like them, keep an eye on the catalogs.

Mustards   Hardy

Various forms of *Brassica rapa chinensis, B. juncea, B. alba, B. japonica,* and *B. pekinensis* (Pak Choy, Bok Choy, Green Wave, Tai Tsai, Mizuna, Tendergreen, Santoh Frilled, Price Choy, etc.)

Technically, some of the varieties I list above are not mustards, but Chinese cabbages. So many of them grow in a leafy form rather than a heading form that I've lumped them together here. Some seed catalogs list them under "Asian greens," which is perhaps a clearer designation.

There are many good mustards for early spring greens. The Japanese are doing a lot of breeding work with them, so you can expect to see plenty of new ones in the years to come. I like to sow them at the same time as the turnips under cold frames at the end of February. When the frames come off in April, I cover the small plants with mosquito netting or Reemay to deter pests. This also shades them a bit, and they grow much leafier than they would out in the open.

Mustards are also good for fall solar-frame work in the colder climates. I don't bother with them in the fall, when there are the Chinese cabbages and so many other bulky brassicas. But they are very useful for small city gardens where the climate is mild. They last well down to 18°F. If you do grow them for fall use, you can start in late August and sow till October. The August sowing needs to be protected from the cabbage maggot.

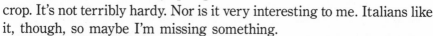

Pak choy

Raab/Rapa   Hardy

Brassica rapa ruvo

This is a small mustardlike brassica that is sown in late August/early September for an early-spring crop. It's not terribly hardy. Nor is it very interesting to me. Italians like it, though, so maybe I'm missing something.

Raab is like the Asian brassicas in that it's quick-growing and bred for the greens, buds, and flowers. There are quite a few varieties still available that could be tried in the Northwest.

Radish   *Raphanus sativus*   Hardy

China Rose
Black Spanish
Daikon types

European radishes are well known as one of the earliest spring crops and can also be sown under frames if you are anxious to have them for the fall.

The daikon types, which are often longer and larger than carrots, can be sown in July and early August. (These sowings must be protected against cabbage maggots.) They can be stored in the ground till Thanksgiving and in mild areas till Christmas. You can also lift and store radishes in damp sand like carrots. I haven't tried this because I'm not fond of them.

Straddling over the daikon
I pulled it up with all my might:
Its root was small.

—Ginko

Rocket   *Eruca vesicaria sativa*   Half-hardy

Rocket is a small, unselected brassica with a nutty taste reminiscent of watercress but even better. It will grow almost anywhere. It is not especially hardy to frost but will germinate in the wettest and coldest of spring soils. Rocket comes charging out of the ground in a couple of days (hence, I suppose, its name) and shows an admirable ability to obtain phosphorus from cold soils. Weather that makes turnip seedlings look sick is nothing to this brassica. I have taken to sowing a few plants among the overwintering cold-frame lettuces, and then again in midspring.

Below is a response from a friend who read the unenthusiastic comments about rocket in my first manuscript. It is a perfect example of the individuality of tastes and gardens.

> *[Rocket was] my first crop and absolutely delicious despite your disdain! Try it in pocket bread with hummus or in salad with feta cheese and you'll become a convert. The slugs didn't touch it, which I suppose is why it* was *my first crop. (It has beautiful flowers, too!)*
>
> *Judy Munger*

I must admit that I have become rather more fond of it (a good example of how your tastes can change when you have something available in the garden "off season"). The flowers are just as edible and make a big hit in salads.

Rutabaga   *Brassica napus napobrassica; B. napus rutabaga*   Hardy

Laurentian
Altasweet (STK, TER)

Though Altasweet is rumored to be the best, *I* can't tell much difference among the varieties. I found only a limited use for rutabagas because there are so many other winter roots I prefer. But they are fairly hardy and can be grated raw into salads, steamed, mashed, and put in soups and stews. They are also a good crunchy surprise in *kim chee.*

Seakale *Crambe maritima* Very hardy

Lily White (CCS, BARB, BLUM, SUF)

This rather exotic and bitter perennial crucifer grows wild on the seacoasts of Britain. Crowns of it are grown in British gardens or kept in cellars for forcing in the early spring. This produces long white stalks that are used like asparagus or chard (which is often called seakale beet). There are good descriptions of how to do this forcing in Simons and Shewell-Cooper. Seakale is definitely not one of your frontline staples, but a luxury item. I've been too busy to try it, but if you're interested Seeds Blüm carries seakale as of this writing.

Turnip *B. rapa rapifera* Very hardy

There are three main uses for turnips: early-spring sowings for roots and tops; late-summer sowings for storage roots; and late-summer and fall sowings for tops, or "greens."

The catalogs list many varieties for February sowings under frames, which you should try if you like turnips.

The yellow varieties, including Golden Ball, Orange Jelly, and Golden Perfection (the last two are English), are good for fall roots. They store well and are perfectly hardy if left in the ground through the winter. Southerners, who prefer turnip tops for fall and overwintering crops, plant such varieties as Crawford, Purple Top, and All Top. Nutritionally speaking they get the better deal, as there are more vitamins and minerals in the tops than the bottoms. The tops are nutritionally superior to spinach also, and the roots have far more calcium and vitamin A than potatoes. Most catalogs offer some form of turnip; Cook's Garden and Seeds Blüm have a few exotic ones.

Watercress *Nasturtium officinale* Hardy

Watercress (ABL, JSS)

This is found in ditches and streams, even in such cold areas as the Midwest. Watercress is easy to start from either seed or cuttings. If you can get a bunch of it from a farmer at a local market, try rooting it in water or very moist sand. It will produce well in any spot with rich soil that you can keep moist through the summer.

Watercress is not particularly hardy, though when it grows in running water it is protected from light frosts. It crops best in the early spring and fall. It will self-sow like mad if allowed to go to seed in the summer.

In fact, it is so weedy and vigorous and moves downstream at such an alarming rate that I question the wisdom of allowing it in your favorite stream. Sure is good in salads and soups, though!

Onions

Onions are such a wonderful and staple vegetable that it's comforting to know that you can have them all year round—green or bulb, as you prefer.

Garlic   *Allium sativum*   Hardy/very hardy

Silverskin
Red Spanish

If you put garlic cloves in around October, they will put up green shoots just like onions. These are milder than the cloves and go well in salads, sauces, omelets, and so on. Separate the ones for cutting from your main garlic crop, as cutting robs the new cloves that are forming. The larger Red Spanish variety is more vigorous through the winter. It sends up a seed stalk in the early summer.

Leeks   *A. porrum*   Very hardy

I have come to treasure leeks in the last few years. They are so hardy, so tasty, so attractive, and, in our area, not bothered by much. They fill the gap if you run out of bulb onions, and make welcome gifts and trade items. They also have a unique flavor and are good baked, pickled, in soups, and in many other dishes.

They are slow-growing and, like onions, delicate and small for the first two months. It is a good idea to start them in seed beds or flats in April. In June, lift them, trim the tops and roots, and plant them at six to eight inches apart. I can get three or four rows in my 36-inch beds. This gives me slightly smaller leeks, but I prefer them that way.

Like the cabbages and several other winter vegetables, leeks come in fall and deep-winter varieties. As might be expected, the fall varieties are less hardy, but they emphasize height, bulk, and tenderness. They are also often a paler green. The winter ones are stockier, with that dark blue-green color I have come to associate with the hardiest of winter crops. They have a higher dry-matter content and higher mineral and vitamin levels. Today most seed catalogs will help you differentiate between the fall and winter leeks, but 10 years ago this was not always the case.

Nowadays I don't have the space and time for fall leeks, so I can't recommend any new varieties — you'll have to do your own experiments. Among the winter ones, Carentan has been my personal favorite for a long time. This started in the fierce winter of 1978–79, when it had an 80 percent survival rate in the trials. I find it also has a nice flavor and is tender enough for salads, though it doesn't get very large. I rather like this, as I don't enjoy monster leeks. It also has no bulge at the base of the shaft, and so is easier to lift from the soil and to clean. But most years I try a few of the new hardier leeks just to compare them. They always seem very good. Maybe some day I'll find something to supercede Carentan.

Overwintering onions *A. cepa*   Very hardy

Walla Walla Sweet
Winter Sweet

In the northern part of our range, these hardy types are sown in a seed bed at the very end of July or in the first week of August. Once

they are large enough (the end of September, usually), you can plant them out at a normal spacing to overwinter. Pull them as green onions from about April on. They begin to bulb up in May and are usually ready for harvest as dried bulbs by mid- to late June. It is important to observe the correct sowing date so that they are large enough to make it through the winter but not so large that they bolt the following spring. These are not super keepers, but they will last until your regular bulb onions are ready.

Scallions *A. fistulosum, A. cepa*   Very hardy

The true scallions, *Allium fistulosum*, are non-bulbing perennials, called Welsh onions in England. This misnomer comes from the Old English *Welisc*, meaning "foreign" or "strange," and of course is also the root of the Anglo-Saxons' name for Wales. A typically British ethnocentric slur, but in the case of the onions, appropriate enough, as they seem to have come from Asia. In their original form, they grow in clumps with small, slightly swollen bottoms, and multiply like chives. Known as *cong bai*, they were for centuries the common garden onion of China and Japan, and are considered therapeutic against colds. The Japanese have done a lot of varietal work on them. Some other forms of scallions are actually *Allium cepa*, and these are not hardy, in the main. Some are, and you can use them if you want, but they are not perennial, so you will have to buy seed and sow every year. It's much easier to just maintain a bed of *A. fistulosum*, I think.

Top-set onion

To start off a scallion patch, sow seed any time in spring or early summer. Fall plantings can be made, too. They flower in midsummer and then die down. With the September/October rains, they start growing and are usable again. Growth slows around the solstice, but they are available again until June or sometimes July following a rainy spring. Their flowers, which come on in June, are good for salads.

There are several commercial permutations of the scallion emphasizing different traits. Some aren't hardy, but Evergreen Hardy White, Hardy White Bunching, He Shiko, and White Welsh make it through even New England winters.

Top-set onions   Very hardy

A. cepa proliferum
   Egyptian/Tree onions/Multipliers (ABL)

Although these onions are very hardy and tasty, I have given up growing them. I didn't find them very prolific compared to the hardy scallions. You can propagate them two ways:

1) By top sets, or bulblets (little bulbs that form at the top of the stalk where the flowers should be, or sometimes in coexistence with them).

You can harvest these in midsummer when they are ripe and plant them for greens in the fall. They will then turn into next year's mature onions. The stalks die down, leaving the big bulbs in the soil.

2) Harvest three or four of the big bottom bulbs, leaving one in place to multiply, or harvest them all and select the best to replant for reproduction. These bulbs are strong-flavored and at their best when dug from the soil in midwinter.

Once you have these growing in your garden, you should have them for a long time, as they are very hardy and persistent and don't require much attention, not even weeding. I had top onions in Wisconsin under an old apple tree, where they propagated themselves happily, year after year, surviving temperatures of -30°F and three feet of snow.

Miscellaneous onion family greens for winter
Very hardy

If you are in a hurry and haven't got starts of any of the other types, you can plant onion sets, garlic cloves, or shallots for a supply of greens through the winter. They can be planted any time from early September through October, and pulled for greens as desired.

Other Vegetables

Broad bean/Fava *Vicia faba*
Hardy

Windsor
Windsor Long Pod
Aquadulce

As you can see from the Latin name, favas are vetches and were, along with peas, the legume of choice before the introduction of New World crops. They are decidedly *cool-season* crops (though Johnny's is now listing varieties bred for hot weather) and should be sown as early as possible in the new year. In mild areas a November sowing will work fine, though rot and mice can be problems. A late sowing in March or April is fine if you don't have bean aphid (sometimes erroneously called black fly) in your area. Bean aphids can overwinter on Bigleaf maples; if you have those in your district and they are infested, you should try for a November or January sowing so that you will have well-grown plants by the time the aphids make their appearance in the spring. Then you can just cut back the tender tops which the aphids attack.

In hard-frost areas, where November and January sowings may not survive, try a February sowing and aphid patrols in infested areas (see Sharecroppers).

In either case, favas are ready before the snap beans *(Phaseolus vulgaris)* and *sometimes* before the peas. I think they're best when the seeds are the size of a large thumbnail; later the skin gets tough (though the seed inside still tastes good). Some books recommend eating the pods too when they are the size of small snap beans, but I find them bitter even when that small. The big dried beans are good in soups and stews but need long cooking. At any size, they are a good protein source. And don't forget to try adding a few of the flowers to spring salads!

Beets *Beta vulgaris*   Hardy

Lutz
Winterkeeper (STK)

Winterkeeper and Lutz are the two standard winter beets. I can't find much difference between them. Any of the small beet varieties such as Detroit will do, too.

Beets for keeping should be sown in late June or early July so they have time to mature their big, tender, sweet roots. Both Lutz and Winterkeeper have pale green leaves that taste rather like chard. If you have frosts that go much below 15°F, you should mulch or else lift and store them in a cool place.

Burdock *Arctium lappa*   Very hardy

Takinogawa (ABL, JSS, TSA)

I used to collect burdock wild in the Midwest. The roots and young, tender shoots are strange-tasting but good. The Italians, the Chinese, the Japanese, and Juliette de Baïracli-Levy place great store in its medicinal qualities.

Sow in the spring (it's a slow grower) and gather from fall onwards. However, don't let it go to seed and escape to your land, especially if you keep sheep; it's a pernicious weed, and the burrs will make the wool unusable. Good in soups, stews, and stir-fries.

Cardoons   *Cynara cardunculus*   Half-hardy
also known as *Scolymus cardunculus*

(DAM, RICH)

Cardoons are a tall relative of the globe artichoke, with a similar flavor. In the fall, their stalks must be blanched even higher than celery by wrap-

ping with paper. When blanched in this way, they will stand until December. Simons, the *Oxford Book of Food Plants,* and especially Pellegrini have good descriptions of how to grow these.

Cardoons are sown in May and harvested in November. After the first harvest in the fall, you can let them overwinter for a good final crop in spring. The seeds generally don't mature as far north as Washington State.

I tried growing cardoons and was rather disappointed in them. They took up a lot of space, and I found them fuzzy and bitter; nothing I did seemed to overcome these problems. I was not inspired to try again. If you are, you had better confer with an expert.

Carrots   *Daucus carota sativa*   Hardy

In my first garden in Seattle, I inadvertently left carrots in the ground all winter and they were great till April. Unfortunately, every place I've gardened in the Northwest has been host to plagues of carrot rust flies, nasty relatives of the cabbage maggot. When their larvae attack, they leave behind long, gray- and rust-colored tunnels that make the carrot bitter.

So now I harvest them and store in damp sand or peat. If you don't have rust fly (or wireworm) and want to store carrots in the ground, mulch them well, for they are ruined by temperatures lower than 10°F.

For several years I tried different varieties of carrots for summer eating and storage. One type I tried kept like mad but was rather tasteless.

We ended up not eating it. Then I discovered that my favorite munching carrot stored admirably. I just have to time the sowings so that the storage crop is ready at the first hard frost but doesn't overmature and split. It goes into storage at peak quality and comes out almost the same. By all means, try some of the European storage types, but if you find you don't like them as well as your favorite summer carrot, try the above technique.

Celery *Apium graveolens dulce*   Half-hardy

Utah 52-70
Leaf Celeries

In my Seattle garden, most Utah celery plants overwintered without any difficulty, just a few frozen outer leaves. They tasted very strong and bitter, though, and were most-ly good for soups and stews (but *very* good for that). A few plants lived three years, which surprised me since they are supposed to be biennial. Perhaps it's because I took the center flower stalk to eat before it bloomed.

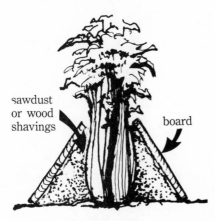

sawdust or wood shavings

board

Celery mulch

At temperatures much below 18°F the centers die out, so if you live in a cold spot and want to carry them over, try a high mulch (or put them in cold frames, cloches, or plastic sheds). If the outer leaves die back before you use them, be sure to take them off. Mushy, rotten stalks will eventually rot the core of the plant. I have not had much luck with mulching regular celery in Whatcom County. I use the hardier leaf celeries instead. I start them along with the celeriac and then put the plants in a protected place, such as a cold frame or a bed against a south wall. Here they are quite happy most winters and produce new leaves from the center as I pick the outer ones.

I have also tried growing the winter celeries that are available in Sut-tons and other English catalogs. For the life of me, I can't see why they bother with them. The ones I tried had tough, bitter leaves like those of celeriac, but no swollen root. They didn't seem as hardy as the leaf celeries, and they were much more fuss to grow. They are supposed to be for blanching by mulching in a trench. I'm afraid I find that too much work.

Celeriac *Apium graveolens rapaceum* Hardy

Blanco (JSS)
Alabaster

Celeriac is one of my favorite winter roots. It's very versatile; tasty in soups and stews, grated fresh into salads, or steamed with a cream sauce. You can use it to replace celery stalk in recipes.

Celeriac needs to be started early in flats and kept in a frame until the weather warms. Up north I start seedlings in April in flats. Since they need a very rich, moisture-retentive soil, I line the flat with a layer of newspaper and then add two inches of fresh or composted cow manure (without any bedding). Then I put in two inches of potting soil and firm it down. The seeds go on top of this and are kept fairly moist both before and after they germinate. They are quite slow-growing, but when they get crowded in the flat, I put them into individual pots. In June, the celeriac is planted out into its permanent home. By using this method I have been able to get big, mature roots by harvest time, even in hard clay soil. I store them dry or in damp sand. In milder districts like the islands or cities, they can be left in the ground. They should be mulched if the temperature drops much below 18°F.

Use treated seed, as celeriac is susceptible to leaf spot (which is also a problem for parsley, one of the best winter greens).

Chickweed *Stellaria media* Very hardy

Chickweed (ABL)

A weed of most gardens, chickweed makes an excellent living green mulch for Brussels sprouts and broccolis, though it can overwhelm lettuce and onions if you have good soil. Chickweed is bothersome in the cool seasons of the year, and in a rainy summer it never dies back. It is a serious weed in heavy soils. Regular and frequent cultivation is the only way to keep it under control. If by some

chance you *don't* have chickweed in your garden, pick it in the fields or from a friend's garden.

The size of the leaf indicates the fertility of the soil—as big as watercress, fantastic! Chickweed grown on rich soils has bigger leaves that are more succulent and have better flavor. I clip the stems with scissors to avoid pulling the lower parts of the runners out of the dirt, and use the plant in salads. J. de Baïracli-Levy says it has medicinal qualities.

Dear Binda,

Did you know that chickweed was still a real vegetable in medieval times? I once read an old guild statute, where all the different courses of a meal were described, which the wife of a Master Craftsman had to serve to the journeymen, and there was also Mierlein, *or chickweed, mentioned. How times change!*

Ute Grimlund
Marysville, Washington

Chicory   *Cichorium intybus*   Very hardy

Root
   Witloof (French endive)
Leaf
   Red Verona   Sugarloaf
   Sugarhat   Greenlof

Chicories are in the same family as lettuce, but these perennials are wilder, slower-growing, and bitter cousins. Like lettuce, they are at their most useful as cool-season crops and are grown in several forms for different purposes. A bitter, coffeelike drink can be made from the roots, special varieties are forced in the dark for sprouts during the winter, and some forms are used for salad greens. Varieties for all purposes are usually sown in the four weeks directly following the summer solstice. In the fall, the leaf chicories are cut for harvest, and in mild areas the roots are left for spring leaves. The roots of the others are lifted, dug, dried, roasted, and ground to make the chicory drink. I find the leaf chicories to be the simplest to grow.

If you are inspired to try the forcing types, read one of the older English gardening books mentioned in Appendix D for complete instructions. Joy Larkcom has a good section on all the chicories in *The Salad Garden.*

You would do well to read this book anyhow for its complete and beautiful treatment of salads.

Briefly, to produce roots for forcing, sow the seed of Witloof (or whatever new variety your favorite seed catalog carries) at the end of June. Thin the seedlings to six inches apart and keep them well weeded, as they are very slow growers. In the fall when you have time, trim off all but an inch or so of the tops and store the better roots in a box in the cellar or a dark part of the shed.

When you want some chicons, as the sprouted tops are called, put a few roots in a box or pot of wet sand. Cover or keep them in a completely dark place. The roots will send up shoots that will be soft, blanched, and elongated because of the darkness. When they are about five inches tall, they can be cut off and eaten. They taste only slightly bitter and have a great texture. They are wonderful in salads. Europeans sometimes cook them, but I haven't tried this. Neither have I taken the time to force the root chicories.

Leaf chicories are sown in June in a fairly good soil and kept weeded. They should be thinned to six inches apart in the row. By late September, they should form heads. You can harvest these as you want until the November rains, or longer if you cover them. They keep for months in the refrigerator in a plastic bag as long as they are free of disease and dry on the outside as they go in. Their bitterness decreases with storage. If you have a mild climate, you could leave them out in the garden; I've taken mulched chicory to -2°F under Reemay. I like the leaf chicories in salads mixed with other greens. They have a great texture. The red-streaked types are especially beautiful.

The older varieties came in many forms—some for big leafy heads, some for small rosette types, some for tight heads with self-blanched centers. Even within a given type there can still be a lot of variation (as is true of many open-pollinated vegetables). If you grow 10 Red Veronas, you might have three or four that don't head. These will be more or less a loss, as the outer leaves will be rather tough. But the other good heads will make the effort worthwhile.

Two of the older varieties that I find immensely attractive are Castelfranco and Palla Rossa. These are variegated forms, green splotched with red and yellow. They are not so bitter and are great to look at in both the garden and the salad.

In recent years there have been some worthwhile additions to the tribe by European breeders, such as the green Sugarhat or Sugarloaf types.

These grow into large romainelike heads whose inner leaves self-blanch to a glorious golden color. They will stand until late October, but are better off after that if harvested and stored in clean plastic bags in the fridge. Here they become even milder and will last three months if they are dry and disease-free when you put them in.

The other breeding innovation has been among the red heading varieties, commonly called radicchio in this country. These have been bred to be more tolerant of varying daylength, so you can, with care, sow them early in the spring and get red heads. (Formerly, the red came on mostly with cooler weather.)

Corn salad/Mâche/Lamb's lettuce   Very hardy
Valerianella locusta olitoria

Large Leaved English
Large Leaved Dutch
Verte de Cambrai
D'Etampes, Elan, Vit, etc.

Garden corn salad was derived from a weed in the "corn" (grain) fields of Europe. It is a three-inch-high plant with a very soft, distinctive flavor.

Corn salad

As it is a winter annual, it germinates after the late-summer or fall rains and over-winters in the rosette form. In spring it puts on a lot of growth, sending out three or four flower stalks from each plant. Although it's small, I think it is one of the better winter crops.

In Holland they have whole greenhouses full of corn salad for market, and consequently there are many Dutch varieties. English and French catalogs also list many types.

I like it in salads from September until the end of April, but it is most useful from January through April, when there is a shortage of salad material. Even in its spring growth spurt, corn salad does not get bitter like lettuce. The flowers are a forget-me-not blue and just as delicious as the rest of the plant.

If you are growing corn salad for the first time, sow it thinly in late July, or just after the first heavy August rains. You can also make a September sowing in milder or more southern parts. I have clumps of it established in my herb beds and just let it go to seed on its own. In the summer I weed once or twice, and later in the summer, as the soil cools down, the seedlings emerge where they will. It's very handy not having to worry about sowing it! If you want to save seed, spread news-papers under the plants to catch the seed, as it ripens unevenly and drops to the ground over a month's time. I just bundle the long, trailing stems together in one spot and let the seed fall. It gets spread around when I clear the bed for the next crop.

The large-leaved English types give you more winter bulk, but I like the flavor of the smaller French variety, so I grow both. Sometimes I suspect, though, that I couldn't tell them apart in a blind taste test!

Dandelion   *Taraxacum officinale*   Very hardy

Another weed, dandelion is very good for helping your body recover from the midwinter doldrums from February through April. You can dig the young plants and steam the greens, or pick the tiny unopened flower buds and eat them raw in salads. The blanched leaves make a very ac-ceptable salad addition, and a cleansing tea can be made from the roots.

Endive/Escarole   *Cichorium endivia*   Half-hardy

Curly endive and the flatter-leaved escarole are good fall and early-winter crops, especially under frames. I prefer the Batavian varieties, as the hearts blanch well and sweeten as winter progresses. They are not hardy, though, and should be kept under glass except in mild areas without much winter rain. If you like to eat the whole head at once, rather than picking the outer leaves, you can blanch (whiten) the plants by put-ting a flower pot over one head at a time. The centers self-blanch to some degree.

Sow endive and escarole in June or early July to get big heads. If you miss these sowings and are going to grow them under cover, you can sow as late as August in the north.

Florence fennel   *Foeniculum vulgare azoricum*   Hardy

Florence Fennel (ABL)

Italian in origin and only recently found for sale outside specialty markets, Florence fennel, or finocchio, is worthy of more attention by local gardeners and cooks. Sown in early- to mid-July, it grows somewhat like celery with a funny, swollen base. Cut off the leaves and eat them raw in salads or steam them, or saute them in a little butter—marvelous and succulent. The root is good, too.

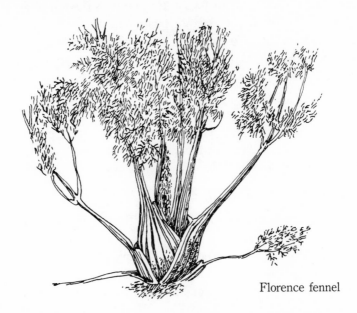

Florence fennel

I avoided Florence fennel at first because I'm not terribly fond of fennel-seed flavor, but this almost disappears in the cooking. The plants will go through several light frosts and last until November in the north (perhaps later in the south or other milder areas).

For non-bulbing fennel, see the Herbs section.

Good King Henry/Mercury   Very hardy

Chenopodium bonus henricus
Good King Henry (RED, COOK, RICH, WELL)

I still haven't grown or tasted this, but like everyone else, I know its relative, *C. album* (known variously as fat hen, lamb's-quarters, and goosefoot), which is an annual weed of the summer garden. Good King Henry is a perennial that shoots up very early in the spring. The stalks can be eaten like asparagus; later, use the leaves like spinach. It will do well in any rich garden soil (in the perennial section, of course).

I suggest buying a live plant (WELL) because I have bought seed and sown it twice to no avail. It's a weed, so until you find out more about its growth patterns, keep it restrained.

Jerusalem artichoke *Helianthus tuberosus* Very hardy

This perennial species of sunflower produces a large quantity of tubers that can be left in the ground all winter. The plants are very weedy and tall; keep them well away from, and to the north of, the rest of the gar-  den. The tubers are good raw in salads or lightly sautéed, but not boiled, as they are even easier than potatoes to overcook.

Get some healthy-looking tubers from a local co-op or supplier. Most seed companies carry them now; some, like Seeds Blüm, have many interesting varieties. They can be planted in the ground any time from October until May, but they won't be ready for eating until the following fall. Then they can be dug as wanted from October until April. The tubers store well in plastic bags in the refrigerator for a month or more. Mice and slugs like them, but the plants almost always produce more tubers than you can possibly eat anyhow.

Lettuce *Lactuca sativa* Hardy

Thanks to the general passion for lettuce, breeders produce many different varieties every year, and many of them are suited to fall, winter, and early-spring production. At this writing, the Cook's Garden has the best (and most amazing) selection of lettuces of all types for every season. It is possible to sow lettuce in any month from February until October, either in cold frames or outside. To have a continuous supply, you only need five or six sowings timed to your situation and microclimate. The Dutch, French, and English breeders have done most of the work with cool-season varieties, and some of the better ones come from them. But several "garden store variety" American ones, such as Oakleaf and Prizehead, also perform well.

Early spring varieties

There are many good varieties for sowing under frames in February.
I sometimes start the seedlings among the overwintered lettuces and
early peas to save on space. Then I move some of them out in April when
the frames are getting crowded and it is warm enough for them to do
well. Good ones I've tried are Kwiek (SUT) (though the catalogs recommend it for fall sowing), Oakleaf, Prizehead, Red Sails, Bibb, Buttercrunch,
the dwarf and rather soft romaine Little Gem (SUT, TER), and May
Queen or King (SUT). Really, this is an easy time to produce lettuce under
a frame; the days are getting longer and warmer, boosting vitality so
much that disease is usually not a problem.

Fall varieties

Sowings in late July and August will provide lettuces for September
through December, and later under frames. These sowings are difficult
ones to get going, due to the summer heat and dryness. If you have a
rainy break, the soil should be cool enough to germinate the lettuce. Otherwise, make your sowings between two and four in the afternoon and water
well. The seed will have the cool night to begin germination. This technique, recommended by Bleasdale and Salter in *Know and Grow Vegetables,*
is based on the particular dormancy response of lettuce seed to heat.
You can also shade the soil.

Good varieties are Little Gem (SUT, TER) for winter cold frames;
Winter Density (JSS), a medium-sized romaine to be covered after Thanksgiving in colder areas; Winter Marvel (Merveille d'hiver), the best butter-
head type that I have tried for fall, with good rot resistance; Prizehead;
and Oakleaf. Many people use Black Seeded Simpson, and English books
frequently mention Valdor, Imperial Winter, and Arctic King.

Whichever variety does well for you, keep it well spaced (on nine-inch
centers) and dust the soil with basalt, volcanic ash, or sulfur to prevent
disease. I find that in the north I have to cover this set of lettuce by mid-
October if I want it to last through the winter. More often, because of
the rot problem, I just let it freeze and go without lettuce until the October-
sown varieties under glass start to produce in March. I guess I enjoy
having a break from lettuce. I focus instead on grated carrots, corn
salad, celeriac, chinese cabbage, and sprouts for my salads. If *you* would
like lettuce at this time and live in an area with frequent hard freezes,
keep some rugs or mats on hand to put over your frames when the
temperature drops.

Overwintering varieties

If you were away in August or were too busy to sow fall lettuce then, you can still make a sowing under frames in September and October that will overwinter and begin to produce extra leaves by early March and whole heads by the middle of April. I find this batch very useful, as I begin to enjoy lettuce again just about this time. Good varieties that may be available include Kwiek, Prizehead, Marvel of Four Seasons, Rouge d'hiver, Pirat, Red Montpelier, Royal Oakleaf, Nancy, and Little Gem. It's very interesting to watch these little lettuce seedlings slowly come up to size through the winter and then race away in February and March to form heads.

New Zealand spinach *Tetragonia expansa* Hardy

I don't grow New Zealand spinach because I'm not fond of it, but those who do tell me that it is as cold-hardy as it is heat-resistant. Apparently, in a mild fall it will last until Christmas.

Parsley *Petroselinum crispum* Very hardy

Parsley is a highly nutritious vegetable and should be in every garden. I find curled parsley too strong-tasting in the heat of summer, but by fall it has sweetened up with the rains and cool nights. The only trouble is that most American varieties are bred for tenderness and won't stand up to later cold weather. The best I've tried are the European varieties from Stokes, Bravour and Darki, which do well all winter.

I am most fond of plain parsley. Sometimes seed catalogs don't make a clear distinction between the small, plain parsley and the very large Italian type (perhaps because the commercial growers don't). The latter grows up to two feet high, almost on the celery level, and has a rather strong flavor. It's immensely productive. I don't find it a very good subject for the winter herb garden, but if you have a *big* family, perhaps you could keep up with it. Plain parsley is productive enough as it is, though it slows down around midwinter. In my garden it has proved hardier than American curled sorts, though it isn't much better than the European winter varieties. If you have a strain of plain parsley that you like, try selecting for winter-hardiness—you could end up with a good thing.

Sowing dates for winter cropping are the same as those for summer use. You can also sow later in June, but you will get smaller plants. I grow most of my parsley in a very well-protected flower bed, where it self-sows. I have both curled and plain, and they look lovely amongst the yellow blossoms. Occasionally I put in a new plant if there aren't enough seedlings.

Parsnip *Pastinaca sativa*   Very hardy
Any variety

Parsnips were the potatoes of Europe before Columbus and all that. Today they are in disregard, but in fact have many uses. They are delicious grated in stir-fries, soups, stews, and cakes, as well as baked or just plain steamed. They are very hardy, though in heavy, wet soil deficient in lime, they are vulnerable to a form of rot called canker. If your parsnips show signs of this, make raised beds, lime well, sow later or closer to get smaller roots, and use resistant varieties such as White Gem (SUT) and Avonresister.

In the north, parsnips can be sown in April or May, and in the south until June or July if you want very small ones. Make sure to keep them well weeded. A mulch helps if you have fine enough material. Parsnips should be planted in a bed that was well dug and manured for a previous crop.

Peas *Pisum sativum*   Not hardy

It is theoretically possible to make a July sowing of peas and get a fall crop just before the fall frosts. The problem is that it is hard to keep these moisture-loving, cool-weather plants going through the rigors of the hottest part of the summer. Even if you do manage this, there is a virus in the Northwest, called pea enation, that will cripple most varieties. A few resistant types have been released. I've tried some of them, and so far I'd say it's not worth the trouble, if you live in a pea-growing district where the enation is rampant. But if you live in an out-of-the-way corner where there is no enation, or not much, and you *love* peas, you might try them. Territorial and Nichols have both carried resistant varieties. Also check with your local extension agent.

Salsify *Tragopogon porrifolius*   Very hardy

I find that salsify, a member of the daisy family, is a good alternative to parsnip. I like it best sautéed or in soup. It isn't super-sweet like parsnips, and it has a very rich flavor. Sow thickly in April (later sowings germinate poorly), water only during droughts, and keep weeded—that's all there

is to it.

In the spring, the new leaves are good cooked or as a salad green. Salsify is a biennial, so if you want to save your own seed, just leave one plant and it will shoot up four to five feet by May and show its purple flowers through June mornings. The seeds come in a ball like dandelions (and are just as weedy), so catch them before they shatter in a wind on dry July days.

Scorzonera *Scorzonera hispanica* Very hardy

Scorzonera, a close relative of salsify, is a perennial with black skin and yellow flowers. The difference in flavor between the two is subtle, and I'm not sure I could tell them apart blindfolded. However, scorzonera does have straighter, longer roots and, in my experience, makes a heavier crop. You can leave it in the ground for two years; the roots just get bigger.

The cultural requirements are the same as for salsify, but I think deep digging would really be merited here. The roots can be up to 18 inches long, so unless your soil is very loose, you will often lose the bottom part when you dig the plant. On the other hand, if the weather or your time and strength don't allow you to dig a bed in April, don't worry. The roots will get down into the subsoil by themselves, drawing up valuable nutrients for you to eat in January and February.

If you also have plantain growing in your

garden, it will be hard to distinguish the two at the seedling stage. The differences are that scorzonera leaves have serrated edges and are downy on the inner surface.

Skirret *Sium sisarum*   Hardy
(WELL, BLUM, SSE)

Skirret is best started from root divisions, but it will come from seed if you get it fresh. It's a member of the carrot family, and the German name, *Zuckerwurzel*, seems to imply some sweetness.

Reports are that you can store the roots in the ground over the winter, or in sand like carrots.

Spinach *Spinacea oleracea*   Very hardy

Cold Resistant Savoy (STK)	Tyee
Giant Winter (ABL, DAM)	Sigmaleaf (SUT)
Winter Bloomsdale	Dixi Market (HAST)

Spinach is amazingly hardy, but you have to provide rich soil with a fairly high pH and a well-drained bed for it to overwinter in. If sown in late July or early August, it will yield a fine fall crop as well as plenty of leaves till about Christmas. Then it rests until March (February in a mild winter) and comes on again. In cold sites, it's best to cover plants from late November until the end of February if you want good production. In an early winter, you could cover it by late October. In northeaster country, a rug thrown over the frames will give added protection when the temperature goes below 15°F. I've had it last to -2°F this way.

I find the savoyed (crinkly leaved) types to be sweeter but not quite as productive as the flat-leaved sorts. So if you have a large family or go in for bulk, try Giant Winter, Sigmaleaf, or a similar sort for cooking. Munsterlander, a German flat-leaved variety that I got through the Seed Savers Exchange, is an extremely productive and fairly sweet winter type. Winter Bloomsdale and Cold Resistant Savoy should be saved for salads.

Spinach needs a cool soil to germinate well, so try to sow in a rainy break. If none is forthcoming, sow in the afternoon and keep well misted, as with lettuce. In very hot summers July sowings might bolt, especially if your soil is not moisture-retentive. Then you can sow again; though you will get smaller plants, you will still have some of this valuable winter crop. Sowings later than August are mainly good for overwintering under glass (or uncovered in a mild district) to provide you an extra-early spring crop. My overwintered spinach always tastes better, looks better, has more bulk, and bolts later than the early-spring sowings (though one year I threw some "old" spinach seed out with the crimson clover seed for green manure and got the best spring crop ever. . .food for thought!).

Swiss chard *Beta vulgaris cicla* Very hardy

Fordhook giant (JSS)
Lucullus (ABL, PARK)
Geneva (PARK)

This is one of the few vegetables that you regularly see overwintering in gardens around the Northwest. It is very popular in Europe, where it is a big commercial crop. (In English catalogs you will find listings of seakale beet or spinach beet, which are similar to Swiss chard but often don't have as big a midrib.)

If you are only growing chard for winter use, then sow it in July. I haven't grown it in years, so below are some comments on chard by my neighbor and first editor, Lane Morgan, who lives in Sumas. She gardens an eighth of a mile from the Canadian border and is hard hit by the devastating northeasters that roar out of the Canadian mountains several times each year.

I like it for its winter bulk and early spring rebound. The ribs aren't good past fall, but the leaves taste nice. Mine dies back in northeasters and I cut it down to a nub so it won't rot. It starts growing again in February and lasts 'til May. Chard lasagna is great. Ruby chard is very beautiful but I have never had any luck with it. [I found it bitter, myself. —B.C.]

I grow Fordhook Giant. Germination is slow and the plants are initially pokey, but after they get going they are indestructible.

Herbs

Herbs merit a section of their own because, being more powerful in flavor, they aren't used in the same large quantities as the other vegetables. But that little bit makes all the difference, especially to your winter and spring salads, sauces, and soups. They haven't been bred to be all soft and puffed up the way we like the rest of our vegetables, so they have more vitamins and minerals in their leaves.

Also, though many perennial herbs die back somewhat in the depth of our winters, they stay late and come back early. Their earliness is especially welcome for meals served in the March and April doldrums. You can disguise cabbage with a Lemon Thyme sauce, or revolutionize the same old salad with new lovage sprouts. Most of the herbs mentioned below are known for their medicinal properties as well as their culinary virtues, another good reason to have them available for winter consumption.

Anise *Agastache foeniculum*   Half-hardy

This tall member of the mint family, with its purple-tinged leaves and lovely lavender flowers, is a welcome addition to fall and spring salads. It is a short-lived perennial, and the leaves are best from seedlings. I have it growing in the edible flower hedge alongside my garden. Here it self-sows happily, and I never have to bother with it until I want to add a few flowers to a fall salad, or some of the soft, anise-flavored leaves from the seedlings. The bees, both honey and native, love the flowers.

Chervil *Anthriscus cerefolium*   Hardy

Another anise-flavored plant, with small lacy leaves, and one that will last all winter, chervil gives a surprising taste to winter salads. It's no

bother, as it self-sows in late summer. To start it off, sow the seeds in good soil in late July or August, and water until the plants are established. If your soil has a lot of winter weed seed in it (chickweed, groundsel, common mallow, and the like), you may have to weed thoroughly, as chervil is not very competitive.

In 1985, when I visited a small

market garden in France's Loire valley near Orleans, they showed me an overwintered turnip-rooted chervil that, even though it was still immature, tasted very good. They called it *cerfeuil bulbeux*. They were going to send me roots in the fall but never did. If you manage to obtain seed, remember that, like many umbellifers, it doesn't last long and needs to be stratified before sowing. A good description of this (or a closely allied vegetable) is given in *The Vegetable Garden* by Vilmorin-Andrieux, but she calls it *cerfeuil tubereux* and classifies it as *Chaerophyllum bulbosum*.

Chinese chives/Garlic chives   *Allium tuberosum*   Hardy
(JSS, WELL, RICH)

Known as *gau choi fa* by the Chinese, this tastes somewhat like garlic. It is relatively new to occidental gardeners and is a perennial that is started from seed. It is very slow-growing and should not be cut until the second year. In following years, divide it regularly to keep its vigor up. The onionlike flowers that appear in late summer are very attractive and good in salads. The leaves are available till late in the fall, much later than chives, but they don't come up as soon in the spring.

Chives   *Allium schoenoprasum*   Very hardy

Chives tend to die down in October or November, especially if it's a dry year. Then they reappear in late February (or even earlier if you lift and force some in a sunny window), so I think they're worth having. The lavender flowers are excellent in salads. Get a root division from a friend or buy a bedding plant in the spring.

Chrysanthemums   Hardy
Chrysanthemum leucanthemum (ox-eye daisy, wild chrysanthemum); *C. morifolium* (garden chrysanthemum, florist's mum); *C. coronarium* (shungiku)

It is good to find cool-season edibles within this genus, seeing as, with the exception of shungiku, we have them around anyway!

Daisies are everywhere, and if you have them as a weed in your garden soil as I do, you will soon notice that they are green and inviting in the fall and spring. I have been eating their pungent little leaves since I lived in the Midwest, and now I throw them into the mixed salads that I make for friends and family.

The flowers of garden chrysanthemums (in their basic white form) have been considered a good medicine for the lungs and liver by the Chinese for quite a while, and they are very nice in fall salads and also as a tea. The leaves are a trifle strong, and so for stir-fries and salad greens I prefer shungiku. Several sowings in the spring and fall will keep you supplied, for a little goes a long way. One plant left to its own devices in the flower border will give you lots of seeds and seedlings without much work.

Coriander/Cilantro/Chinese parsley   Hardy
Coriandrum sativum

This herb is remarkably hardy. March sowings germinate with alacrity, and late August or early September ones will last until January and sometimes until spring in a mild winter, especially under cover. The strongly aromatic leaves can be used like parsley in salads and are common in Mexican, Chinese, and East Indian cooking. The flowers are good in salads and an important food for syrphid flies, a predator you might want to encourage in your garden. Let some mature for the seeds. It will occasionally self-sow.

Fennel   *Foeniculum vulgare*   Very hardy
Seed or root division

A perennial that is around for most of the year, this fennel dies down in October or November and then comes back up early in March. Not everyone will like its strong flavor, but if you do, it's there waiting for you. I have seen quite a few wild plants in different parts of Seattle. They get very large (three feet in diameter and four to five feet high) and should be planted where they won't interfere with your other herbs. Fennel is a very assertive plant and hard to eradicate, so weed out volunteers diligently.

Bronze fennel is a far more restrained garden herb—and its leaves and flowers are a great visual hit in salads. For bulbing fennel, see Other Vegetables.

Horseradish   *Armoracia rusticana*   Very hardy

You can dig the root of this crucifer all winter, if you remember to. In the spring, the pungent new leaves are a treat in salads. Horseradish is very easy to grow from a piece of root crown; in fact, it's hard to kill, so be sure to put it where it won't take over the rest of your perennial herbs. Rumor has it that workers in horseradish processing plants don't get colds very often—like vampires and garlic, maybe?

Lovage *Levisticum officinale* Very hardy

This member of the carrot/celery family is a perennial and has a wonderful, unique taste. It makes an early spring or fall salad, soup, or sauce into something special. I got my plant by root division from a German winter gardener, but it apparently comes easily from seed. Try to get seed fresh in that year; it ripens in July/August. The University of Washington's Medicinal Herb Garden has a nice bunch of plants.

Miner's lettuce Very hardy
Montia perfoliata (sometimes called *Claytonia perfoliata*)

I never really noticed this persistent native until I started making "wild" or "seasonal" salads. Then its small, cupped bracts and lovely pink-and-white flowers caught my attention. It *does* look lovely in a salad mix and is available from early spring to late fall. But it has a rather bitter aftertaste. So use with discretion, perhaps just as a garnish.

Mints *Mentha* spp. Very hardy

Peppermint and spearmint emerge from the soil in the early spring with the most beautiful little sprouts that taste surprising in salads but are only usable for a short period. Variegated lemon balm, a member of the same family, starts early and goes on late into the fall, and its yellow and green variegations as well as its lemon taste are a wonderful combination with limestone lettuce, butterheads, or in a mixed wild salad. If you want to try Scotch mint (also available in a variegated yellow form), confine it in a tub or pot. It's an incredible weed. I'm still trying to eradicate it from my yellow flower bed after three years. It doesn't really have that good a flavor, either.

Oregano *Origanum* spp. Variable hardiness

The pink-flowered oregano, though tough and very hardy, doesn't have much flavor. The white-flowered wild oregano, *Origanum vulgare,* has proved hardy in my garden, but the seed is hard to find. Check Richters and Well-Sweep for Greek oregano. While this is not too hardy, it is truly super-strong!

Primrose   *Primula vulgaris*   Very hardy

In the spring of 1984, the owner of Log House Plants in Cottage Grove, Oregon, gave me a whole flat of blooming primroses—such a gift of joy! I took what I could home on the plane and dug them into the semi-shaded southern side of a cedar tree in my new abode. Here they have happily expanded and presented me with cheerful flowers for my salads both late into the fall and first thing in the spring. Some very mild years they bloom almost all winter. The yellow ones, perhaps because they're closest to the species form, have lasted the best.

Rosemary   *Rosmarinus officinalis*   Hardy

From cuttings

It's best to get a cutting of this, put it in a fairly dry, sunny place, and water well until it's established. Rosemary is wonderful in winter stews, and small bits of the leaves or flowers are good in salads. It also makes a soothing tea after a long excursion in the rain.

Sage   *Salvia officinalis*   Very hardy

Most Americans know this in its dried form. It grows easily and you can have it fresh most winters, too. The variegated form is pretty and surprising in salads.

Salad burnet   Very hardy
Poterium sanguisorba (sometimes called *Pimpinella saxifraga*)

Salad Burnet (ABL)

I feel that this is an herb of borderline usefulness. It certainly stays green throughout the winter, and it does taste of cucumbers, but rather bitter ones, unfortunately. Though it isn't very succulent, it does offer a nice variation in your winter salads, and it's supposed to be very good for you. Sow in spring or summer. Cows are said to relish it.

Shepherd's purse *Capsella bursa-pastoris* Hardy

This tiny common cruciferous weed has a pretty inflorescence early in the spring. It is considered nutritious and therapeutic, and looks good in salads. In some mild autumns, the summer-germinated plants will also send up flowering stalks.

Sorrel Very hardy

Rumex scutatus
  French Sorrel
  Garden Sorrel
R. acetosa
  Grande de Belleville

R. acetosella
  Wild sorrel

Plain

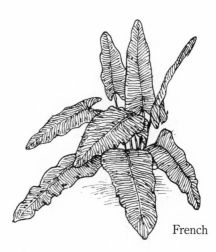
French

The sorrels impart a wonderful sour flavor to salads, but you pay for it with oxalic acid. I guess a certain amount of this doesn't hurt you, and if you aren't into lemons they are nice plants to have.

I had a German roommate in high school who said her family made a soup of wild sorrel during World War II called *Saueramfer Suppe*. The small leaves are good in spring salads.

Thyme *Thymus vulgaris* Very hardy

German Winter Thyme
Lemon Thyme (*T. pulegioides* X *T. vulgaris*)
Caraway Thyme (*T. herba-barona*) (WELL)

Common thyme is found in many gardens, so you should be able to get a division. Variegated lemon thyme, which is so good in winter salads, is less common and you might have to search a little harder for it. It isn't as hardy in its first two years and might need mulching lightly in a cold site. Caraway thyme is fairly hardy and good in salads and herb butters. German winter thyme is a plain sort that stays greener in the winter.

Valerian   *Valeriana officinalis*   Very hardy

In the early spring, valerian plants put forth many deeply cut purple leaves. These are quite good in salads, and their color is welcome at that time of year. Valerian is known for its soothing properties, so some might be useful after a hectic day. Start from seed or get plants.

Violets   *Viola* spp.   Hardy to very hardy
(STK, WELL, PARK, RICH)

Wild violet flowers and leaves are edible and high in vitamin C. The Swiss and winter-flowering pansies (*Viola hyemalis*) and heart's-ease, or Johnny jump-ups (*V. tricolor*), bloom early and late and make nice additions to salads. The leaves of the latter taste of wintergreen. Sweet violet (*V. odorata*) leaves are edible but bitter. The flowers have an amazing Victorian-style perfume. All the violets provide a visual treat in the herb border as well as in salads.

Wintergreen/Teaberry   *Gaultheria procumbens*   Very hardy

This is a lovely little perennial ground cover of the northern coniferous woodlands that adapts well to similar environments here. It likes open shade and acid soil. I have it growing on the west side of a cedar, well mulched with wood shavings. The wintergreen-flavored April and May blooms are delicious for sweets such as fruit salads or homemade ice cream. The new growth is bright red, and so are the berries that come in late summer and are available until you, the birds, or the mice eat them. They will last under the snow. Buy plants.

Winter savory   *Satureja montana*   Hardy

In my experience this is a short-lived perennial of variable hardiness. It tastes rather like thyme, but is not as attractive or vigorous. I had better luck with it in Seattle than farther north.

APPENDIX A

GARDENING OUTSIDE THE MARITIME NORTHWEST

Introduction

Some areas of North America that lack a true maritime climate still have mild enough winters to grow crops through most of the year. In Florida, the Gulf coasts, and southern California, year-round cropping is well established. In other areas, such as northern California, Appalachia, and the south Atlantic coast, many gardeners are not aware of the potential for overwintering and winter production. If you live in one of these areas, this section will acquaint you with *some* of the possibilities available to you.

If you live in eastern Washington or Oregon, you will be facing a winter similar to that of the northeastern states and would do well to read some of the books recommended for that area.

California

The northernmost part of California, especially along the coast, is really maritime Northwest in climate. Although the timing may be a little advanced from southern Oregon, you are still following a basic maritime pattern of cool summers and moist, mild winters. Inland, the mountains and river valleys of the Klamath, like the Rogue, lead to such topographical complexities that it is useless for me to generalize.

Farther south, in the Mendocino area, there is a good local book available to guide you. James Jankowiak's *The Prosperous Gardener* covers year-round gardening for that region. The Farallones Institute Rural Center in Occidental is available to help you with questions. SLUG (see

Appendix C) is also a good source.

Informants tell me that the limiting factor for crops in the lowlands of northern California is not low temperatures so much as pests and diseases. As these are less prevalent during the winter, it is a good time to focus on the more vulnerable plants. Useful books for this area include *How to Grow More Vegetables* and *The Self-Sufficient Gardener.* But the two best, I think, are the *City People's Book for Raising Food* by Helga and William Olkowski, and Robert Kourik's *Designing and Maintaining Your Edible Landscape Naturally.* The Olkowskis are the people who helped start the Integral Urban House, and their book is well worth reading. It is a model of intelligent thought and action as well as good gardening experience (see Appendix D). Kourik's book, which is all of the above, is also very extensive and the current bible for this general area on the subject.

Ecology Action of the Midpeninsula has developed designs for a "multi-use mini house." Similar to a cold frame, this structure can be used during the summer months to shade and protect from pests those cool-season plants that need to be started during the summer.

I have not been able to find out too much about winter cropping in the coastal ranges and the foothills and higher elevations of the Sierras. I imagine that they are rather like the Alps, the Apennines, and the Pyrenees—in other words, an elevated Mediterranean climate. One would do well to look toward Swiss, Spanish, and Italian seed sources. Gardeners from those areas might have useful information. This is also true for the coastal lowlands.

Northeastern U.S.

Although New England cannot be said to have mild winters, quite a lot of experience has been gathered there by gardeners growing crops in cold frames and solar greenhouses. In 1977, Helen and Scott Nearing brought out their book on sun-heated greenhouses, which described their experiences overwintering leeks, lettuce, endive, chard, and parsley in Maine. A 1981 book from Stephen Greene Press, *Intensive Gardening Round the Year,* is an extensive coverage of gardening techniques, including an excellent chapter on cold-season gardening under various frames. Most of the information comes from the authors' experiences in New Hampshire and Vermont. See Appendix D for these titles.

The Rodale group in Pennsylvania has experimented with overwintering greens in solar cold frames (usually well reported in *Organic Gardening* magazine) and has several publications of interest to the year-round gardener in colder climates.

All of these sources supply reading lists and information on relevant seed companies. See Appendix C for addresses.

Southeastern U.S.

Many areas in the southeast are suitable for winter crops. In fact, some vegetables, such as spinach, collards, and kale, are grown there in the winter by commercial truck farmers.

There are two main impediments to regular and reliable winter cropping. One is the heat of the summer, which encourages insect pests and inhibits the growth of many of the heat-sensitive maritime vegetables. The other is that storms from the coldest parts of the continent often bring sudden, severe winter weather even to the coastal strip. Both of these problems can be dealt with, but it takes a bit of extra time and energy and probably limits crops and varieties to those that can be most easily protected.

Late sowing, shading, and screening are probably the most effective defenses against summer heat and insects. A large modular structure that can be fitted over beds would probably serve well; the design developed by Ecology Action of the Midpeninsula might be useful (see Appendix C). When cold weather threatens, the screening can be replaced by glass or fiberglass panels, and mats or rugs can be placed over the frames to further insulate them during very severe cold spells.

The best crops for this intensive frame culture are the cut-and-come-again greens such as spinach, green onions, dwarf kales, herbs, lettuce, endive, and the Asian brassicas. I have spoken to gardeners from the southeast coast and the Appalachians who have successfully carried over these crops, so if you are interested in fresh greens for much of the winter, give them a try!

See Appendix C for the addresses of useful groups in the southeast.

Planting Times for Coastal Bay Area

Artichoke	August–December*** or plant seed in February	Kohlrabi	July–August
Asparagus	January–February***	Leek	February–April
Beans—snap	May–July	Lettuce (leaf)	December–August or later
Beans—fava	November February–April	Lettuce (cos)	March–April
Beets	February–August	Mustard	February–March July–August
Broccoli	February–March June–September*	Onions	January–March***
Brussels sprouts	April–July	Parsley	December–May
Cabbage	January–October*	Parsnips	May–June February or fall
Chinese cabbage	July–August	Peas	January–August November
Carrots	January–August	Peppers	May**
Cauliflower	January August–September	Potatoes (Irish)	January–August***
Celeriac	March–June	Pumpkins	May–June
Celery	February–May August–September	Radish	All year
Chard	February–May	Rhubarb	December–January
Chayote	January–March***	Rutabaga	July
Chives	February–April	Spinach	August–March
Corn (sweet)	April–July 15	Squash (summer)	May–July
Cucumbers	May 1–July 15	Squash (winter)	May–June
Eggplant	May**	Jerusalem artichokes	January–March***
Endive	March–July	Sunflower	April–July 15
Garlic	October 15–February***	Tomatoes	April–May**
Kale	January/February September/October	Turnips	January–February August

* Plants only after August 1   ** Plants
*** Root, set, or other non-seed start often used

This chart was developed by Pam Pierce when she was president of SLUG. She has been an active community garden organizer in the Bay Area since 1976.

APPENDIX B

WINTER CROPS FOR LIVESTOCK

Introduction

When I undertook the care of animals, I was excited to find that there are as many foods available to them in the winter as there are to me— hay, grain, and poor winter pasture are not the only possibilities for livestock. After doing some reading and observing chickens, ducks, sheep, and goats through the winter, I saw that just as my diet had been restricted by the dictates of the supermarket, so theirs had been limited by what was available at the local feed store and by the recommendations of those who sell pasture mixtures.

I believe that the physical well-being of your livestock is certainly as important as your own, whether you keep just a few rabbits and chickens in your back yard or have a flock of sheep, a herd of goats, or a cow on pasture. You have a special responsibility to provide for your animals. They are restrained from wandering at will and cannot select what they need to meet the nutritional requirements of their yearly cycle.

As I see it, the problem is one of habitat. Most livestock species originated in Eurasia and fed on the vegetation of that area throughout their evolution. The native vegetation of the maritime Northwest is *not* similar to that of mid-Europe. Our vegetation is mainly coniferous, and in many places it lacks elements crucial for stock, such as abundant meadowlands, shrubbery, and extensive deciduous woodlands, all of which are diverse in plant and animal species.

When pastures were established on the clearcut forest soils in the maritime Northwest, they were unavoidably created from mixtures bought at the feed store. What's more, these pastures were established during the rise of modern "scientific" agriculture, so the seed mixtures were monotypic, lacking in the important forage plants that might otherwise have been available throughout the winter. Native hedgerow plants do seed in along fence rows, but they were (and still are) often rooted out.

What can you do to reverse this unhealthy trend for your stock? You can study the lists in this section and the books recommended in Appendix D to increase the diversity of the natural feed available for your animals. Not only will your animals be healthier, but in the end this approach might even lower your feed costs a bit, since most of the species listed are perennial plants.

Emphasis on higher production for greater profit has led not only to stockpiled food, but also to extreme stress on those organisms doing the production (that includes you, too!). In the homestead situation, you do not usually *need* to force your animals to produce those extra gallons of milk or whatever, and they will probably be happier and longer-lived for your not doing so.

I have divided the winter-feed suggestions into three categories: succulents (such as kale), pasture plants (herbs, legumes, and grasses), and browse (hedgerow plants with their buds, catkins, bark, fruit, and nuts). There is also hay (beyond the scope of this book) and what David Mackenzie, author of *Goat Husbandry*, calls "concentrates."

Concentrates are condensed proteins and carbohydrates, available in such foods as milk powders, grains, soybeans, linseed cake, and other by-products of agricultural industries. They are very rich and, I think, not all that suitable in the diets of animals except in small amounts or at particular stress points through the year. Browse, in fact, is a natural form of concentrates. Allowing your animals to eat from hedgerows gives them access to nutrients that various perennial plants produce.

Succulents

Succulents include all the leavings of your garden, plus specially planted stock foods such as marrowstem and thousand-head kale, mangels (a fodder form of sugar beet), sugar beets, turnips, rutabagas, and carrots. The roots are mostly suitable for ruminants (and pigs, to some degree), but the kales and the leavings of your garden are liked by poultry, rabbits, and pigs as well. Succulents can provide a source of fresh vegetable feed for your animals throughout the year.

Pasture plants

If you are raising livestock on an average Northwest pasture, you will want to renovate it as soon as you have money and time. When you do this, include as many herb seeds as you can with the grasses and clovers you choose.

These herbs greatly increase the value of forage and hay available to your stock during the most stressful times of the year—summer drought, winter, and early spring. Many herbs are deep-rooted and collect minerals that grasses and clovers do not, reducing the need for mineral supplements. They are a real asset and are well worth both the extra expense of the seed and the effort that may be required to obtain them.

The three best authorities that I know on the subject of herbs and pastures are David Mackenzie, *Goat Husbandry;* Frank Newman Turner, *Fertility Pastures;* and Juliette de Baïracli-Levy, *The Complete Herbal Handbook for Farm and Stable* (see Appendix D). The Baïracli-Levy and Turner books give lists of plants especially beneficial to different stock. Turner deals mostly with common herbs ("weeds") and their role in pastures. Baïracli-Levy deals with the more medicinal plants for hedgerows and pastures.

This is what Mackenzie has to say on the importance of herbs in pastures:

> *For centuries we have been feeding our sheep and cattle on a mixture of grass, legumes, and miscellaneous fodder plants, including weeds such as daisy, buttercup and nettle, acceptable meadow species like plantain and yarrow, and cultivated pasture plants like chicory and burnet. During all of that time every farmer who wasn't stone blind knew his stock ate most of them and liked them. Until relatively recently he maintained these species on his fields by sowing out with barn sweepings. Since the introduction of pedigree seed mixtures, the average annual hay crop has shown no significant increase, the sale of mineral mixtures for stock-feeding has risen from near zero to over 40,000 tons per annum, and mineral deficiency disease has become a major farm problem. The effect of replacing these miscellaneous pasture plants by grass and clover is to reduce the mineral content of the sward by approximately 20 percent.*
>
> *No special inspiration or insight into the Workings of Nature is needed to reach these conclusions. Brynmor Thomas and fellow research*

workers at the Durham University School of Agriculture have investigated accurately the earlier suggestions of R. H. Elliott and Stapledon. Here are the facts concerning one of their trial fields at Cockle Park.

The Percentage Composition of the Herbage from Swards Containing Varying Percentages of Other Fodder Plants

Constituent	Standard Grass and Clover Mixture	With 10% Other Fodder Plants	With 50% Other Fodder Plants	With 100% Other Fodder Plants
Crude protein	16.75	17.19	16.90	16.94
Crude fiber	21.32	19.49	18.61	15.16
Total ash	10.18	11.07	13.01	14.83
Calcium	1.15	1.36	1.60	2.16
Phosphorus	0.29	0.36	0.38	0.41
Magnesium	0.42	0.45	0.48	0.52
Sodium	0.08	0.11	0.14	0.18
Chlorine	0.26	0.30	0.37	0.48

(David Mackenzie, *Goat Husbandry*, pp. 153, 157.)

Browse from hedgerows

Hedgerows are a form of fence, and they are best used as such. Aside from their nutritional aspects, they provide shelter from the wind for your stock and wildings. They are also a year-long entrancement of plants, birds, insects, reptiles, and mammals, which helps increase the diversity of your local ecosystem. If you have no room for a woodlot, hedges can also be planted with fuel species for coppicing and can serve as an auxiliary herb garden for some of the wilder species of medicinal plants.

Like everything else, hedgerows require some planning, labor, and money to establish and maintain. Depending upon the variety of plants used, the available soil fertility, and moisture, they may take from four to eight years to reach a significant size. Competition from existing weeds, such as thistles, quack grass (also known as couch or twitch grass), the bunch grasses, and blackberries, will be serious unless measures are taken to deal with them.

Whether your planting will be done piecemeal or all at once, soil

preparation is best begun in the previous year. Spring tilling and summer harrowing will kill most
of the quack grass and thistles. A late-summer sowing
of an overwintering green-
manure crop will improve the
soil fertility. This crop can be
turned under in the spring,
followed by a sowing of a
short groundcover grass, such
as a creeping red fescue, along
with any available flower
seeds. The best short-grass
mixture I know of is called
Companion, a mixture of 80
percent Elka, a slow-growing
turf-type perennial ryegrass,
and 20 percent Ensylva, a

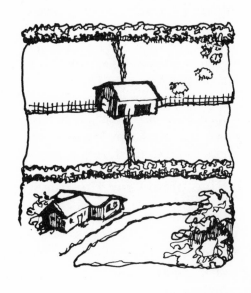

creeping red fescue. It was developed for orchards and is available from
Hobbs and Hopkins Ltd. (see Appendix C). An alternative is 100 percent Kentucky bluegrass. This might be good to mix with herb plants.

Creeping red fescue and the dwarf ryes are short enough to need mow-
ing only around young hedge plants, and will prevent the establishment
of most annual weeds. A quick check several times a summer will serve
to eliminate those few that do enter the row. Or you could prepare a spot
for new hedgerow plants by putting down a mulch of black plastic or
cardboard. Many busy people with long boundaries to hedge set the plants
right into the plastic and leave the mulch there for several years until
the plants have settled in. If you do this, it is best to also lay down a
soaker hose or irrigation hose with emitters at each plant. This will save
your plants from drought and get them up and away quickly.

Stock-hedge plants should be fenced for protection from animals when
small, but planted close enough to the fence to grow through so that they
can be eaten as desired. The animals will keep the hedge pruned on their
side, but you will have to take care of the rest. This trimming, best done
when the stock will benefit from the extra rations, will also make the
hedge denser. For advice on trimming (or laying, as it is called in England),
see John Seymour's *The Complete Book of Self-Sufficiency* or *Hedgerow*
by Thomas and White.

I list below a few shrub and tree species, both native and imported, that are most useful in the edible winter hedge. The starred ones are recommended by Mackenzie as especially good for cool seasons. You can refer to Baïracli-Levy for medicinal herbs. For native shrubs, Arthur Kruckeberg's *Gardening with Native Plants of the Pacific Northwest* is excellent (see Appendix D).

If you are short on cash, read up on plant propagation. As you drive around, keep an eye out for suitable shrubbery. Most people who have a nice plant are happy to share a few clippings. Some of the best winter plants can also be started from seed.

Hedge plants for the maritime Northwest

This list doesn't include the many plant varieties good for summer use. An asterisk (*) indicates the best midwinter plants.

Apple/Crabapple *Malus* spp. The fruits are very good for stock in the fall. Twigs in winter, prunings in spring.

Ash* *Fraxinus* spp. There is a native Oregon ash which is rare in Washington but seems to grow in every swale of the Willamette Valley. If you live up north and have trouble finding seedlings, you can buy one of the eastern U.S. or European species from a nursery.

Beech *Fagus* spp. The nuts are a traditional fall stock-fattener. You probably need two for good pollination.

Birch *Betula occidentalis*. Native hedge plant in eastern Washington. Good for spring and fall.

Blackthorn *Prunus spinosa*. European. Buy from a nursery or get cuttings from a friend.

Blueberry *Vaccinium* spp. Blueberries are hard to propagate and rather expensive from nursery catalogs, but they are fairly easy to transplant. However you get them, they need acid soil and some form of nitrogen, a mulch of sawdust, and plenty of moisture during the growing season. Wild blueberries are good; they can be found in the Cascade foothills (see Huckleberry).

Brambles *Rubus* spp. Raspberries and blackberries. If you *do* plant these, remember that they spread like mad and have to be controlled. Use the native species, as the imported Himalayan and cut-leaf blackberries are already taking over western Washington. Thornless blackberries might be suitable. Use starts from your own plants if you have them. Useful in winter and early spring.

Chestnut *Castanea* spp. Nuts are used to fatten stock (especially pigs) in fall and are wonderful in the human diet, too.

Elder *Sambucus canadensis, S. nigra.* The first is a native east of the Cascades, the second is a European import. Get seed, or try root divisions or seedlings.

Elm* *Ulmus* spp. Easy and vigorous.

Hawthorn *Crataegus monogyna, C. oxyacantha.* These are the European native species. Don't get the cultivars with double flowers—they don't set fruit. You can still occasionally find native black-fruited hawthorn *(C. douglasii)* by roadsides, etc.

Hazel *Corylus cornuta.* A native that can be found everywhere. Highly nutritious; good in early spring, February/March. A relative of filberts *(C. avellana),* which are easy to grow from seed.

Heather* *Erica* spp. English horticultural varieties are available from nurseries. Excellent browse from autumn to midwinter. They are difficult, as they need special growing conditions, such as an acid soil and a weed-free environment.

Holly* *Ilex aquifolium.* European. Common here as both an ornamental and a commercial crop. Goats devour it with glee all winter (and summer, too!). Easy and vigorous, but awfully prickly.

Honeysuckle *Lonicera periclymenum caprifolium.* Introduced. Good goat fare; makes hedge denser by twining through it. This is the common sweet-smelling honeysuckle so often planted. Vines root easily. Goats *might* also like the orange-flowered native, *L. ciliosa* (hummingbirds certainly do), which is much harder to propagate.

Huckleberry *Vaccinium ovatum.* Common evergreen huckleberry, sometimes called box blueberry. Bears dark blue berries until late December. Common on Vashon Island in deep woods. Red huckleberry, *V. parvifolium,* is common in the foothills, where it often grows from old cedar stumps. Sheep like the leaves.

Ivy* *Hedera helix.* Imported; common and easy to start, but hard to get rid of! Good all winter. The berries on mature plants are poisonous to people and many gardeners are irritated by handling the leaves, but goats love ivy.

Maple *Acer* spp. Pigs and cows appreciate the sweet leaves in the fall. Cows and goats will eat the bark and twigs all year.

Mountain ash *Sorbus* spp. Sheep like the leaves; ducks, chickens, and
wild birds like the berries.

Willow* *Salix* spp. Provides good winter feed for cows, sheep, and goats.
The earliest-blooming native willows give bee forage in February.

APPENDIX C
SOURCES
AND RESOURCES

Seed Companies

Nowadays, if I can find what I want, I mostly order from two or three companies. It simplifies my life. But when you are starting out, reading many seed catalogs is almost as educational as reading many gardening books. And for rare varieties or plants you often have to search about a bit.

Some of these catalogs come from outside our growing area. I list them because they have one or more endangered or interesting varieties suitable for the cool seasons. If a variety *is* endangered, it behooves you to see if it is useful to you. If it is, try to maintain seed stock. An excellent way to keep on top of this is to join the Seed Savers Exchange or buy its *Garden Seed Inventory*, which has a complete listing of seed companies in the U.S. and Canada that still carry open-pollinated varieties. I have learned a lot from the inventory. Have fun!

Abundant Life Seed Foundation, P. O. Box 772, Port Townsend, WA 98368. Untreated open-pollinated and heirloom seeds, no hybrids. Many seeds locally grown. Good folks. Catalog $1, membership ($5–$15) includes newsletter.

John Barber Ltd., 2 St. Andrew St., Hertford, SG14 1JD, England. A small company that does not regularly ship overseas but will send the odd packet if you can't get a variety elsewhere.

Bountiful Gardens, Ecology Action, 5798 Ridgewood Rd., Willits, CA 95490. Distributor for Chase Seeds, England.

Buckerfield's Ltd., Box 1030, Abbotsford, BC, Canada V2S 5B5. No U.S. or mail-order, but all you Lower Mainland gardeners can watch for this company's seeds in local stores.

Chase Compost Seeds Ltd., Benhall, Saxmundham, Suffolk, England. Organically grown seeds; winter-hardy varieties and some unusual ones for the rest of the year. Recommended by some International Federation of Organic Agricultural Movements members. The catalog offers pasture herbs in agricultural quantities. Bountiful Gardens (above) distributes Chase seeds in the U.S.

The Cook's Garden, P. O. Box 65, Londonderry, VT 05148. Epicurean vegetables and culinary herb seed. The company claims to have the "world's largest selection of salad greens," and I'm ready to believe it. Catalog $1.

William Dam Seeds Ltd., P. O. Box 8400, Dundas, ON, Canada L9H 6M1. Good Dutch fall and winter varieties. Untreated seed. Recommended.

Gleckler's Seedsmen, Rt. 3, Metamora, OH 43540. Seeds from all over the world.

The Grain Exchange, 2440 E Water Well Rd., Salina, KS 67401. The Exchange publishes its own list in cooperation with Seed Savers Exchange. See entry under Organizations (below) for more details on the group. Garden Grains catalog $1.

H.G. Hastings Co., Box 115535, Atlanta, GA 30310. Strongly oriented to the home gardener; lots of suggestions for early-spring and late-fall gardens for the southeastern states. Free catalog.

Heirloom Gardens, P. O. Box 138, Guerneville, CA 95446. Catalog $2.

Herb Gathering Inc., 5742 Kenwood, Kansas City, MO 64110. This company took over J.A. Demonchaux and, according to Kent Whealy, "his collection is still intact." Catalog $2.

J. L. Hudson Seedsman, P. O. Box 1058, Redwood City, CA 94064. California orientation, but some rare and useful seeds for our area. Catalog $1.

Island Seed Mail Order, P. O. Box 4278, Stn. A, Victoria, BC, Canada V8X 3X8. Inexpensive and reliable flower, vegetable, and herb seed, specifically grown for the Northwest climate.

Johnny's Selected Seeds, 299 Foss Hill Rd., Albion, ME 04910. Untreated seeds, many grown organically on the company's farm. Specializes in short-season varieties, some from Europe. One of the more intelligent and reliable of the northern seed companies. Lots of cultural information. One of my favorites for summer varieties, too. Free catalog.

Kitazawa Seed Co., 1748 Laine Avenue, Santa Clara, CA 95051. Oriental varieties.

Lagomarsino Seeds, 5675-A Power Inn Rd., Sacramento, CA 95824. Interesting northern California seeds, some Italian varieties. Free catalog.

Le Jardin du Gourmet, West Danville, VT 05873. Shallots and some gourmet seeds. Catalog 50 cents.

Le Marché Seeds International, P. O. Box 190, Dixon, CA 95620. In flux, but still carrying some Vilmorin seeds and other interesting worldwide varieties. Free brochure.

Nichols Garden Nursery, 1190 North Pacific Hwy., Albany, OR 97321. Herbs and rare seeds. Now carrying more maritime-oriented varieties. Doesn't make full use of the great range of European-bred seeds, but has many unusual varieties.

Park Seed Co., Inc., P. O. Box 31, Greenwood, SC 29647. Mostly flowers but many interesting ones that northern East Coast companies don't carry because they won't overwinter in continental climates. *Some* vegetables good for winter cropping. Free catalog.

Redwood City Seed Co., P. O. Box 361, Redwood City, CA 94064. Some interesting and unusual vegetables and herbs. Recommended by California gardeners. Catalog $1 (order catalog each year).

Richters, Box 26, Goodwood, ON, Canada L0C 1A0. The mecca for unusual herb seed. If you can't find it anywhere else, try here. Catalog $2.50 (Canadian).

Sanctuary Seeds/Folklore Herb Co. Ltd., 2388 West 4th Ave., Vancouver, BC, Canada V6K 1P1. A good assortment of medicinal and culinary herb seed.

Seed Savers Exchange, Rt. 3, Box 239, Decorah, IA, 52101. A seed-sharing group. Well worth joining for the information alone, but the varieties available are amazing and usually found nowhere else. The winter yearbook reports on conferences, seed-saving tips, and other fascinating details. Membership $16 per year. Send an SASE for publications brochure. The *Garden Seed Inventory* (2nd ed., 1988) is $17.50 paperback; the *Fruit and Nut Inventory* is $18. The organization has 770 members listing over 5,000 varieties.

Seeds Blüm, Idaho City Stage, Boise, ID 83706. Heirloom seeds and other garden gems. A fast-growing company into saving our genetic heritage. Wide selection of good varieties that are hard to get elsewhere. Catalog $3. Has a separate fall planting catalog for the Columbia plateau region.

Shepherd's Garden Seeds, 6116 Hwy. 9, Felton, CA 95018. A good selection with careful instructions. Catalog $1.

Stokes Seeds, Inc., Box 548, Buffalo, NY 14240. Established quality company; wide selection for home and commercial gardening; comprehensive seed-starting directions. Some treated. Free catalog.

Suttons Seeds Ltd., Hele Rd., Torquay, Devon, England TQ2 7QJ. The Stokes of England. Many interesting hardy varieties. *In spite of airmail and exchange rates* you get your money's worth of seed. Order catalog (50 cents) every year.

Tansy Herb Farm, Box 1126, Stn. A, Surrey, BC, Canada V35 4P6. Run by John Balf, who sells plants each weekend in the Granville Island Market in Vancouver; these can be taken over the U.S. border as houseplants as long as they're in sterilized soil. No mail orders at present; if you're in the area, call (604) 576-2785 for directions to the farm. It's best to call ahead rather than drop in.

Taylor's Herb Gardens, Inc., 1535 Lone Oak Rd., Vista, CA 92084. Live plants and some seeds. Catalog $1.

Territorial Seed Co., P. O. Box 27, Lorane, OR 97451. "Garden seed that grows west of the Cascades." Started in 1979, Territorial is working assertively at collecting and breeding maritime-adapted varieties (for both winter and summer) and running trials on them in Lorane and London, Oregon. Current research director and breeder Tim Peters is very helpful with seed-saving questions for our area. Canadian gardeners should write to Territorial Seeds Canada Ltd., P. O. Box 46225, Stn. G, Vancouver, BC, Canada V6R 4G5.

Thompson & Morgan, P. O. Box 1308, Jackson, New Jersey 08527. A rather overwhelming and expensive listing, but occasionally there are some unique vegetable varieties useful to gardeners in a maritime climate.

Tillinghast Seed Co., P. O. Box 738, La Conner, WA 98257. Tillinghast has been serving the Northwest since 1885. The owners are carrying more locally adapted modern varieties.

Tsang and Ma International, Box 294, Belmont, CA 94002. Oriental varieties. Asian brassicas useful for both spring and fall harvests and cloche or cold-frame planting. Free catalog.

Vermont Bean Seed Co., Garden Lane, Bomoseen, VT 05732. Now carrying other flower, vegetable, and herb seeds. Free catalog.

Well-Sweep Herb Farms, 317 Mt. Bethel Rd., Port Murray, NJ 07865. Live plants and dried flowers. Good for those herbs that cannot be reliably started from seed. Catalog $1.

Wyatt-Quarles Seed Co., P. O. Box 739, Garner, NC 27529. Tested and southern-adapted old-time varieties.

Dr. Yoo Farm, P. O. Box 290, College Park, MD 20740. Oriental vegetables. Free catalog.

Suppliers

Cloud Mt. Farm, 6906 Goodwin Rd., Everson, WA 98247. Locally adapted fruit and nut trees, small garden trees, shrubs, vines, and ground covers. Catalog full of good information for our area. Classes offered.

Forest Farm, Ray and Peg Prag, 990 Tethrow Road, Williams, OR 97544-9599. A wonderful array of natives and ornaments shipped in 2″ x 2″ x 6″ containers so you get them young and inexpensively. Catalog $2.

Gardens Alive! Safe Products for a Healthy Garden from the Natural Gardening Research Center. Hwy. 48, P. O. Box 149, Sunman, IN 47041. Nice, informative catalog. For listings of other sources for biological pest controls, see Appendix 9 of Robert Kourick's *Designing and Maintaining Your Edible Landscape Naturally.*

Green Earth Organics, 9422 144th St. E, Puyallup, WA 98373-6686. Natural garden and farm supplies for the Pacific Northwest. Solid, practical tools, supplies, and soil amendments, with no nonsense. Reasonable prices. Also carries territorial line of seeds. Biological and natural pest controls.

Harmony Farm Supply, P. O. Box 451, Graton, CA 95444. Extensive line of irrigation supplies, soil amendments, biologicals, tools, seeds, books, etc. Write for catalog.

Hobbs and Hopkins Ltd., 1712 SE Ankeny, Portland, OR 97214 (tel. [503] 239-7518). Source for the Companion short-grass (dwarf) mixture recommended in Appendix B.

Horticultural Tool and Supply Catalog, A. M. Leonard, Inc., 6665

Spiker Rd., Piqua, OH 45356 (tel. 1-800-543-8955).

Indoor Garden Supply Inc., 911 NE 45th, Seattle, WA 98105. Source of Safer's Insecticidal Soap.

Natural Agricultural Products from the Heart of the Columbia River BioRegion, 333-B Ohme Gardens Rd., Wenatchee, WA 98801 (tel. 1-800-332-3179). Soil tests, integrated fertility management, biologicals, etc.

Walter F. Nicke, Box 667g, Hudson, NY 12534. More garden tools.

Picken & Son Ltd., Frankford St., Works, Birmingham, B19 2YL, England. The only source I know for the original Chase cloche wires.

Raintree Nursery, 391 Butts Rd., Morton, WA 98356. Fruit, nuts, and berries for the Pacific Northwest. Everything for the edible landscaper, and then some!

Smith & Hawken Tool Co., 25 Corte Madera, Mill Valley, CA 94941. Excellent garden tools; books from England and elsewhere.

Stocote Products, 4909 West Rt. 12, Richmond, IL 60071. Supplier of Fabrene. The minimum order is $50, so this might be best as a group buy with your gardening friends. Write or call for prices.

Tolowa Nursery, 360 Stephen Way, Williams, OR 97544. Fruit and nut trees, berries, and woodlot plants.

Weall and Cullen Gardeners Supply Inc., 400 Alden Rd., Markham, ON, Canada L3R 4C1. The company's catalog is subtitled *Innovative Gardening Solutions* and offers lots of good stuff. Associated in the U.S. with The Gardener's Supply Company, 128 Intervale Rd., Burlington, VT 05401.

Whole Earth Access Catalog, 2950 Seventh St., Berkeley, CA 94710. Grain-milling equipment, unusual cooking utensils, and heaps more.

Organizations

Bio-Integral Resource Center, P. O. Box 7414, Berkeley, CA 94707 (tel. [415] 524-2567). This wonderful non-profit organization, started by William and Helga Olkowski, answers members' questions on least-toxic pest controls. It also publishes the quarterly *Common Sense Pest Control* (for lay people) and the monthly *IPM Practitioner* (for keeping the professional updated on recent innovations, suppliers, and resources in the field of integrated pest and disease management). I find the former most useful for my own reading and for showing relevant articles to friends, neighbors, and clients who have problems with specific pests (everything from slugs and aphids to termites and fleas). A catalog listing BIRC's publications is available for $1 and contains membership information.

City Farmer, Suite 801, 318 Homer St., Vancouver, BC, Canada V6B 2V3 (tel. [604] 685-5832). Focusing on urban agriculture and the politics of good gardening. Sponsors education courses, newsletter, an "ability garden" for disabled gardeners, and other projects.

Henry Doubleday Research Association, Ryton-on-Dunsmore, Coventry, CV8 3IG, England. $10 a year for membership. Source for books and rare seeds.

Ecology Action of the Midpeninsula, 2225 El Camino Real, Palo Alto, CA 94306. Distributor of John Jeavons's book. Puts out a "self-teaching miniseries" and various other materials. Largely oriented to warm areas (in other words, California).

Farallones Institute, 15290 Coleman Valley Rd., Occidental, CA 95465.

The Grain Exchange, 2440 E Water Well Rd., Salina, KS 67401. This, with Garden Grains, is a combined project of the Land Institute and project director Thom Leonard. Very interesting for those of you who want, and have room for, a "bread patch" or who just want to keep track of what's going down with your "staff of life." Worthy of support! Basic membership: U.S., $10; Canada and Mexico, $15.

International Federation of Organic Agricultural Movements, Okozentrum Imsbach, D-6695 Tholey–Theley, West Germany. IFOAM is an international umbrella organization with group and individual members, all concerned with the promotion of environmentally sound agriculture. Most European countries have IFOAM members—you can get a list from Rodale (see below). If you wish to correspond with any group or member, you may, but please remember that most of them are volunteers and busy people with few monetary resources.

Rodale Press, 33 East Minor St., Emmaus, PA 18098. Publisher of *Organic Gardening* and source for many studies on gardening techniques.

San Francisco League of Urban Gardeners (S.L.U.G.), 2540 Newhall St., San Francisco, CA 94124.

Solar Survival, Box 250, Harrisville, NH 03450. Plans for solar pods, cones, etc. Reprints of some useful books.

Tilth Association, 4649 Sunnyside N, Seattle, WA 98103. Tilth is a
non-profit association in the Pacific Northwest which links urban and
rural people devoted to a sustainable regional agriculture. Tilth
members are active in growing food, saving farmland, developing
local markets, improving forest practices, and doing whatever they
can to contribute to regional agriculture and forestry. This book was
originally made possible by the Tilth Association, which first published it.

Tilth chapter activities include social events, farm tours, work ex-
changes, research projects, demonstration gardens, conferences, and
farmers' markets. More importantly, the groups work to create a new
agriculture in the Pacific Northwest.

In recent years, Tilth has disassembled its umbrella organization. If
you are interested in getting personally involved, seek out the chapter
nearest you. Your local gardening center should have information,
or contact the Seattle office. Many of the chapters have their own
newsletters and sponsor workshops and other exciting projects. Below
is a partial listing of the chapters:

Olympia Tilth
1827 4th Ave. E
Olympia, WA 98506

South Coast Oregon Tilth
P. O. Box 155
Broadbent, OR 97414

Oregon Tilth
89226 Knight Rd.
Veneta, OR 97487

South Whidbey Tilth
P. O. Box 252
Langley, WA 98260

Portland Tilth
6288 N Interstate
Portland, OR 97217

References for gardeners in the Northeastern U.S.

Rodale Research Center, RD1, Box 323, Kutztown, PA 19530. Partly
owned by Rodale Press (which has a reader service with a current
list of local organic gardening and farming groups), the center re-
searches *Organic Gardening*. You can ask for copies of the press's
numerous articles and research papers on cool-weather crops and
solar structures.

Maine Organic Farmers and Gardeners Assoc., P. O. Box 188, Hallowell, ME 04347. Important and active regional group for the advancement of biological agriculture.

References for gardeners in the Southeastern U.S.

Carolina Farm Stewardship Association, Graham Center, Rt. 3, Box 05, Wadesboro, NC 28170. Emphasis on commercial production.

Piedmont Organic Growers, Rt. 2, Mt. View Rd., Taylors, SC 29687.

Rural Advancement Fund, P. O. Box 1029, Pittsboro, NC 27312 (tel. [919] 542-5292). This very active group has two divisions. Some of the staff members are involved with small family farm, sustainable-agriculture issues such as foreclosures, etc. The rest of the staff work on international policy issues relating to the loss of genetic diversity. They advocate better and more seed storage facilities for vegetable, grain, fruit, and nut crops. Send for information on their *Seed and Nursery Directory*, which is in its third edition. They also offer articles on biotechnology and its socio-economic impact on agriculture and health in the Third World. The staff wrote the January 1989 issue of *The Laws of Life* (available for $18 to non-profits, $33 for all others from the Fund; for readers outside the U.S. the issue can be obtained from the publisher, the Dag Hammarskjöld Foundation, Ovreslottsgaten #2, S-7520, Uppsala, Sweden).

Virginia Association of Biological Farmers, Rt. 3, Box 213, Rocky Mount, VA 24151.

APPENDIX D

FURTHER READING

Books

Aquatias, A. *Intensive Culture of Vegetables: The French System.* London: L. Upcott Gill, 1913. Aside from the explicit hot-bed building directions, this is a very detailed guide to intensive vegetable production under frames. Good photos and drawings in the general chapters, plus an 82-page monthly calendar of planting and other operations. Whole chapter on melon cultivation under frames. Well worth it for the devoted intensive gardener. A 1978 reprint is available from Solar Development Association (see Appendix C).

Baïracli-Levy, Juliette de. *Common Herbs for Natural Health.* New York: Schocken Books Inc., 1974. Once you have the trees, shrubs, and vines of your hedgerow planted, you might want to use this book for ground-cover suggestions.

_____ . *The Complete Herbal Handbook for Farm and Stable.* Rev. ed. London: Faber and Faber, 1984. A Rodale Press paperback reprint is also available. This book is an invaluable aid to weaning yourself and your stock from standard allopathic Western medicine.

Belanger, J.D. *Soil Fertility.* Waterloo: Countryside Publications, 1977. A very good introductory book on soil fertility from the organic point of view. Some overview of European methods and a basic, practical outlook.

Berrisford, Judith. *Gardening on Chalk, Lime, and Clay.* London: Faber and Faber, 1963; Plymouth: Latimer Trend & Co., 1978. Good discussion of soil chemistry and varieties that survive on the respective soil types. Handy reference if you have problem soil.

Bleasdale, J.K.A., D.J. Salter et al. *Know and Grow Vegetables* and *Know and Grow Vegetables 2*. London, New York, Toronto: Oxford University Press, 1979, 1982. Two fascinating volumes jam-packed with basic information, all supported by years of careful research at the National Vegetable Research Station in Warwickshire, England. *Very useful* for maritime gardeners. Order from Oxford University Press, 200 Madison Ave., New York, NY 10016.

Brooks, Audrey, and Andrew Halstead. *Garden Pests and Diseases*. New York: Simon and Schuster, 1980.

Browse, Philip McMillan. *Plant Propagation*. New York: Simon and Schuster, 1988. Published in cooperation with the Royal Horticultural Society. Though not nearly as complete as Hartmann and Kester's *Plant Propagation,* this is one of the easiest books to read on this subject, with step-by-step illustrations of methods.

Chan, Peter. *Better Vegetable Gardens the Chinese Way: Peter Chan's Raised Bed System*. Rev. ed. Pownal: Garden Way, 1985. The author has a wry sense of humor that appeals to me, and the photographs show another culture's version of raised permanent beds. Some winter cropping information.

Doscher, Paul, Timothy Fisher, and Kathleen Kolb. *Intensive Gardening Round the Year*. Brattleboro: The Stephen Greene Press, 1981. A really useful book for would-be year-round gardeners in continental climates.

Fish, Margery. *Gardening on Clay and Lime*. Newton Abbot: David and Charles, 1970. Better in many ways for actual directions for dealing with these soils, though the chemistry is not as good as that in Berrisford.

Fitter, Richard, Alastair Fitter, and Marjorie Blamey. *The Wild Flowers of Britain and Northern Europe*. New York: Scribner & Sons, 1974.

Harrison, S.G., G.B. Masefield, and Michael Wallis. *Oxford Book of Food Plants*. London: Oxford University Press, 1969, 1973. Good reference, gorgeous illustrations.

Hartmann, Hudson T., and Dale E. Kester. *Plant Propagation: Principles and Practices*. 3rd ed. Englewood Cliffs: Prentice-Hall, 1975. The best and most complete book on this subject.

Head, William. *Gardening Under Cover*. Seattle: Sasquatch Books, 1989. A handy guide to building solar greenhouses, cold frames, and cloches.

Hills, Lawrence D. *Grow Your Own Fruit and Vegetables.* London: Faber and Faber, 1975. For more experienced gardeners. Half of the book is devoted to the organic culture of vegetables in a northern maritime climate. Hills is the director of the Henry Doubleday Research Association.

_____. *Organic Gardening.* New York: Penguin Books, 1981. A very good basic book, quite modern, with a minimum of organic "romance" and a maximum of experience. Hills's 40 years of horticultural experience comes across on every page. Very usable in the maritime Northwest, where crops, pests, and diseases are very similar or identical to those of Britain.

Howes, F.N. *Plants and Beekeeping.* Winchester: Faber and Faber, 1979. A new edition of the 1945 classic. Read this to know what to plant to make your hedges and garden a bee's paradise.

Jackson, Wes, Wendell Berry, and Bruce Colman, eds. *Meeting the Expectations of the Land: Essays in Sustainable Agriculture and Stewardship.* San Francisco: North Point Press, 1984. Highly recommended.

Jankowiak, James. *The Prosperous Gardener: A Guide to Gardening the Organic Way.* Emmaus: Rodale Press, 1978. You'd never know from the title that this is such a regional book, focused strictly on coastal northern California. Very pertinent for its area, though, and well worth reading.

Jeavons, John. *How to Grow More Vegetables Than You Ever Thought Possible on Less Land than You Can Imagine.* Rev. ed. Berkeley: Ten Speed Press, 1982. Devoted to the "biodynamic/French intensive" method of raised-bed gardening. Needs lots of adapting to fit maritime Northwest conditions.

Koepf, H.H., B.D. Petterson, and W. Shaumann. *Bio-Dynamic Agriculture.* Wyoming: Bio-Dynamic Farm, 1976. A very lengthy book and not always easy to understand. Worth reading only for the serious horticulturist.

Korn, L., B. Snyder, and M. Musick, eds. *The Future Is Abundant: A Guide to Sustainable Agriculture.* Seattle: Tilth Association, 1982. Lots of information about regional horticulture. A plant species index to help you determine where to place plants in the environment. Out of print; check libraries.

Kourik, Robert. *Designing and Maintaining Your Edible Landscape Naturally.* Santa Rosa: Metamorphic Press, 1986. Written from the

Californian point of view, but still a useful book for all climates, especially the West Coast.

Kruckeberg, Arthur R. *Gardening with Native Plants of the Pacific Northwest: An Illustrated Guide.* Seattle and London: University of Washington Press, 1982. Well worth buying and treasuring. Covers propagation.

Larkcom, Joy. *The Salad Garden: Salads from Seed to Table; A Complete, Illustrated, Year-Round Guide.* New York: Viking Press, 1984. This is a wonderful book, accurate and beautiful, by a happy vegetable fanatic. A real treat.

Levitan, Lois. *Improve Your Garden with Backyard Research.* Emmaus: Rodale Press, 1980. The first chapter is the best part of this book, to my mind. Better review it in the library or bookstore carefully. Still, it's the only book of this sort that I've seen for the lay gardener/researcher.

Lockeretz, William, ed. *Environmentally Sound Agriculture.* New York: Prager Scientific, CBS Inc., 1983. Selected papers from the 1982 IFOAM conference in Cambridge, Mass. Good stuff, even for gardeners.

Lovelock, Yann. *The Vegetable Book: An Unnatural History.* New York: St. Martin's Press, 1971. Strange and amusing poems and descriptions of common and uncommon vegetables.

Mackenzie, David. *Goat Husbandry.* Rev. ed. London: Faber and Faber, 1980. Another of Faber's classic agriculture books, first published in 1956. Fantastic scope and detail, worth it even if you don't have goats. Pertinent to the care of any grazing animal.

McCullagh, James C., ed. *The Solar Greenhouse Book.* Emmaus: Rodale Press, 1978. I don't have a greenhouse yet, but it looks like this would be a useful book.

Mooney, Pat Roy. *Seeds of the Earth: A Public or Private Resource?* London: Canadian Council for International Co-operation and the International Coalition for Development Action, 1979. Even though 10 years old, an excellent précis on the international seed situation.

Morash, Marian. *The Victory Garden Cookbook.* New York: Alfred A. Knopf, Inc., 1982. A wonderful array of vegetable recipes and cultural directions, from the television show "Crockett's Victory Garden." Good for learning how to prepare unfamiliar vegetables and for finding new ways to serve familiar ones.

National Academy of Sciences, *Toxicants Occurring Naturally in Foods.* 2nd ed. Washington, D.C.: National Academy of Sciences, 1973. Compiled by the Committee of Food Protection, Food and Nutrition Board, and National Research Council. If you are into the finer points of nutrition, this book will answer questions and lay to rest myths about toxicants in some of the vegetables mentioned in the text.

Nearing, Helen and Scott. *Building and Using Our Sun-heated Greenhouse: Grow Vegetables All Year Round.* Charlotte: Garden Way Publishing, 1977. A very good book for areas with severe climates or cold spells. Simple, straightforward descriptions with lots of photos of cool-season crops.

Nieuwhof, M. *Cole Crops: Botany, Cultivation and Utilization.* London: Leonard Hill Co., 1969. Very "textbooky," but some revealing information on the more common of the coles. Good if you have to write a term paper and need a reference. Lots of data from studies on low temperatures, pests, manuring, etc. Available from CRC Press, Inc., 2255 Palm Beach Lakes Blvd., West Palm Beach, FL 33409.

Olkowski, Helga and William. *The City People's Book for Raising Food.* Emmaus: Rodale, 1975.

Pellegrini, Angelo M. *The Food-Lover's Garden.* New York: Alfred A. Knopf, Inc., 1970. This is a discursive, interesting book by an excellent Seattle gardener, with general cultural information, recipes, and more. Discusses rocket and chicory as well as cardoons. If you can't find the original, look for the 1975 reprint issued by Madrona Publishers in Seattle.

Philbrick, Helen, and Richard B. Gregg. *Companion Plants and How to Use Them.* Old Greenwich: The Devin-Adair Co., 1966.

Pieters, Adrian. *Green Manuring: Principles and Practice.* London: John Wiley and Sons, 1927. Out of print, but the most complete and interesting book on green manuring. Get it from your local agricultural library.

Pollard, E., M.D. Hooper, N.W. Moore. *Hedges.* New York: Taplinger Publishing Co., 1975. Comprehensive work on the nature and effect of hedges on landscape and farming, including notes on history, flora, fauna, the farmer's hedge, and more.

Polunin, Oleg. *Trees and Bushes of Europe.* London, New York, Toronto: Oxford University Press, 1976. A goody for naturalists and those who wish to understand more about introduced European plants.

Seymour, John. *The Self-Sufficient Gardener: A Complete Guide to Growing and Preserving All Your Own Food.* Garden City: Doubleday, Dolphin Books, 1979. Though the vegetable-growing directions are a bit scanty, the overall scope is good for those who like the visual approach. Includes fruits, hedgerows, livestock, etc.

Shewell-Cooper, Wilfred Edward. *The Basic Book of Cloche and Frame Gardening.* London: Barrie & Jenkins Ltd., 1977. This is one of the best English books on types of frames and year-round use. Now out of print. If you find a second-hand copy, buy it! Better than any new West Coast information.

_____. *The Complete Vegetable Grower.* Winchester: Faber and Faber, 1975. I like this book even better than when I read it the first time in 1975; I've experimented and learned a lot since then, and now I can appreciate it more. It was written by a professional English horticulturist. One of the better modern sources for maritime gardeners.

Simons, Arthur John. *The New Vegetable Grower's Handbook.* Markham: Penguin Books Canada Ltd., 1975. An encyclopedic listing of vegetable crops and when to grow them. Quite useful but hard to get.

Smith, Miranda, and Anna Carr. *Rodale Garden Insect, Disease & Weed Identification Guide.* Emmaus: Rodale Press, 1988. An important tool for the gardener. The forerunner to this guide, *Rodale's Color Handbook of Garden Insects* by Anna Carr (1979), has better plates for some insects.

Solly, Cecil. *Growing Vegetables in the Pacific Northwest.* A self-published classic from the forties, now out of print and available only in libraries.

Solomon, Steve. *Growing Vegetables West of the Cascades: A Guide to Natural Gardening.* Seattle: Sasquatch Books, 1989. Recently revised, this popular book by the former owner of the Territorial Seed Company contains much valuable information for organic gardeners.

Storl, Wolf D. *Culture and Horticulture: A Philosophy of Gardening.* Wyoming: Bio-Dynamic Farm, 1979. Written in the Rogue Valley of Oregon, this is the most modern of the "BD" books. An interesting (though a bit slanted) history of the organic movement in general and the BD one in particular. A pretty out-front discussion of their unusual concepts of cosmology.

Sunset Books and *Sunset* magazine editors. *Attracting Birds to Your Garden.* Menlo Park: Lane Publishing Co., 1975. Fairly good coverage of Northwest species.

_____ . *Sunset New Western Garden Book.* 4th ed. Menlo Park: Lane Publishing Co., 1979. The general encyclopedia-type book for this area.

Thomas, Eric, and John T. White. *Hedgerow.* New York: William Morrow & Co., 1980. A very pretty book and a good, though short, introduction to the history, botany, wildlife, and folk uses of hedgerows in England.

Thomas, Graham Stuart. *Colour in the Winter Garden.* 3rd rev. ed. London: J.M. Dent, 1984. This is about ornamentals, but once you achieve year-round vegetable-gardening consciousness, you might want to extend your joy in this direction. One of my very favorite books.

Thompson, H.C., and W.C. Kelly. *Vegetable Crops.* New York: McGraw-Hill, 1957. *The* college textbook on veggies, from Cornell. Now in its umpteenth edition.

Turner, Frank Newman. *Fertility Pastures and Cover Crops Based on Nature's Own Balanced Organic Pasture Feeds.* San Diego: Rateaver, 1975. Faber and Faber reprint of the 1955 classic. Good book about increasing and maintaining fertility through the use of green manures and special pasture mixes for leys (temporary pastures), which can serve as part of the large-scale rotation of crops on farms. Emphasizes various grasses and herbs. Focused on feed for cows.

Vilmorin-Andrieux, M. M. *The Vegetable Garden: Illustrations, Descriptions, and Culture of the Garden Vegetables of Cold and Temperate Climates.* First published in England in 1885. Berkeley: Ten Speed Press, 1981.

Westcott, Cynthia. *The Gardener's Bug Book.* 4th ed. New York: Doubleday & Co., 1973. Good for descriptions of various insects, but ignore the chemical use recommendations.

Yanda, William, and Richard Fisher. *The Food and Heat Producing Solar Greenhouse.* Santa Fe: J. Muir Publications, 1980.

Pamphlets

Colebrook, Binda. *Vegetable Gardening Almanac.* Everson: Maritime Publications, 1983. A 19-page, year-round almanac featuring month-by-month gardening directions and variety recommendations. Includes suppliers listing and chart showing nutrients in common vegetables. Updated biennially.

Cooperative Extension Service. *Beneficial Predators and Parasites Found on Washington Crops.* Washington State University, 1975. Bulletin #640.

_____ . *Garden Insect Control without Synthetic Insecticides.* Washington State University, 1973. EM 3757.

_____ . *Guidelines for Manure Application in the Pacific Northwest.* Washington State University, 1976. EM 4009.

Hills, Lawrence D. *The Vegetable Finder.* Braintree: Henry Doubleday Research Assoc., 1977. A listing of the better-flavored older varieties that are getting hard to find in Britain. Write for an updated version. The HDRA is also maintaining a seed bank of "discontinued" varieties that, though they cannot be sold under current EEC rules, can be given away.

Johnston, Robert, Jr. *Green Manures: A Mini Manual.* Albion: Johnny's Selected Seeds, 1983. Available from Johnny's Selected Seeds.

_____ . *Growing Garden Seeds.* 2nd edition. Albion: Johnny's Selected Seeds, 1983. Available from Johnny's Selected Seeds.

Kourik, Robert, Edible Landscape Project. *Graywater Use in the Landscape: How to Use Your Graywater to Save Your Landscape During the Drought.* Santa Rosa: Edible Landscape Project, 1988. A little encouragement toward doing what you ought to do anyway: water shrubs and flowers with the dishwater. (It saves on the water bill!) Order from the Edible Landscape Project, P. O. Box 1841, Santa Rosa, CA 95402; $6 postpaid.

Labine, Pat, George Burrill, and James Nolfi. *The Home Grown Vegetarian.* An analysis of homegrown food and diets. Order from the Center for Studies in Food Self-Sufficiency, 109 S Winooski Ave., Burlington, VT 05401.

Miller, Douglas C. *Vegetable and Herb Seed Growing.* Hershey: Bullkill Creek Publishing, 1977.

Say, J. S. *Gardening on Difficult Soils: Clay, Sand, and Peat.* London: A. H. Reed, 1977. Very nice, concise pamphlet. Available through interlibrary loan.

Schmid, Otto, and Ruedi Kläy. *Green Manuring: Principles and Practice.* Obervil: Institute of Biological Husbandry, 1981. The first edition of this was published by Faber and Faber (London) in 1976; D. Kindersley Ltd. (London) reprinted it in 1977. A very interesting discussion of the qualities of many green manure species as used in Switzerland. Available from Woods End Agricultural Institute, Old Rome Rd., Box 1850, Mount Vernon, ME 04352.

Weinsteiger, Eileen. *Summary of Cool-Weather Crops Tested 1979–80 for Solar Structures.* Emmaus: Rodale Press, 1981. Published by the Horticulture Department of Rodale Research Center (see Appendix C). If you like to grow greens and salad crops under frames, read this.

See also entry for Bio-Integral Resource Center, under Organizations in Appendix C.

Periodicals

The Cultivar. Published twice a year by the Agroecology Program, College Eight, University of California at Santa Cruz, Santa Cruz, CA 95064 (tel. [408] 429-4140). Lots of fascinating information on innovative trials of intercropping, native American farming and gardening techniques, various local agriculture efforts, and the agroecology program itself. Though a bit out of our area, it's worth examining this for the quality of the thinking behind the activities—it could serve as a model for efforts in our rainy and cooler northern clime. Free.

HortIdeas. Rt. 1, Box 302, Gravel Switch, KY 40328. A monthly periodical abstracting horticultural information of interest to horticulturists at all levels. Highly recommended. Subscriptions: second-class U.S. mail, $15; first class, $17.50.

Maine Organic Farmer and Gardener. Box 2176, Augusta, Maine 04330. A well-written, informative monthly tabloid.

INDEX

honeysuckle, 123
horseradish, 70, 108
hot beds, 40–41
huckleberry, 123
Hungarian turnip, 82

"integrated pest management,"
43–45
ivy, 123

Jerusalem artichoke, 99

kale, 80–82; 2, 6, 11, 12, 17, 19, 21,
31, 45, 66, 70, 72, 75, 115, 116,
118 *passim*
kohlrabi, 82
Kourik, Robert, 114

lacewing larvae, 45
lady beetles, 45
lamb's lettuce, 96–97
Larkcom, Joy, 31
Latin square, 59, 62
leeks, 86–87; choosing varieties
of, 17, 18; cultivating for seed,
20–21; 2, 11, 12, 21, 28, 58, 66,
72, 80, 114 *passim*
legumes, 10, 11, 118
lemon balm, variegated, 109
lettuce, 99–101; 2, 5, 6, 24, 27, 28,
29, 33, 35, 58, 114, 116 *passim*
light, effects of on garden, 5–6
livestock, winter crops for, 117–124
lovage, 109
lupine, 11, 13

mâche, 96–97
Mackenzie, David, 119
malathion, 45–46
mallow, common, 106
manure: animal, 9, 14, 15, 40, 41,
45; green, 9–11, 120; seaweed, 45
maple, 123
Master Gardeners, 24, 43
mercury, 98–99
metaldehyde, 56, 61
mice, 43
mildew, downy, 58
miner's lettuce, 109
mints, 109
mountain ash, 123
mulches, 9, 12–13

Musick, Mark, 31
mustards, 82–83; 10, 13 *passim*

nematodes, predatory, 52
nicotine spray, 45
Nieuwhof, M., 74
nitrogen, 11, 13
northeastern U.S., winter gardening
in, 114–115
Northwest, map of, 4

oats, 10, 11
Olkowski, Helga and William, 114
onions, 86–98; greens, 6, 89; 28,
58, 66, 116 *passim*
onions, overwintering, 11, 87
onions, top-set, **88**–89
open-pollinated varieties, loss of,
19, 20
oregano, 109
organic gardening discussed, 16
parsley, 101–102, 114; Chinese, 108
parsnip, 102; 2, 19, 21, 28, 58, 72,
80 *passim*; wild, 54
pasture plants, 119–120
pea enation, 102
peas, 102; 28, 33 *passim*; as green
manure, 11
pests, 43–61. *See also* individual
pest names
Philbrick and Gregg, 62, 63
phosphorus, 13
plantain, 103
pod cold frames, 38
potatoes, 33, 57
potassium, 13
primrose, 110
Puget Sound, climate, 23
pup tent cold frames, 38
pyrethrum, 44, 57–58

Queen Anne's lace, 54

raab, 83
radicchio, 96
radish, 11, 47, 83–84
rapa, 83
Reemay, 51, 53, 82, 95
rocket, 33, 70, 84
Rogue Valley, 24
root canker, 58
rosemary, 110

Binda Colebrook was born in England and raised on Cape Cod, Massachusetts. She first learned about gardening from her mother, who is both a professional writer and a lifelong gardener.

Binda earned a degree in social anthropology from Radcliffe and a master's degree in environmental interpretation from the University of Wisconsin. Her thesis was a guide to the Arboretum Prairies. In Wisconsin she taught classes in foraging for wild foods for the local co-op, explored the  woods, rivers, and prairies, and gardened in her spare time.

After moving to Seattle in 1971, Binda continued her involvement with co-ops, gardened in the city's first P-Patch, and worked at Earth Station 7 and the Country Doctor Community Clinic. She soon discovered that the mild maritime winters of Seattle made it possible to grow fresh vegetables year-round, and she wrote about her findings in the first edition of *Winter Gardening*, published in 1977.

Currently Binda works as a landscape gardener in and around Bellingham, Washington, and lives with her 15-year-old son in Everson. She publishes the *Northwest Maritime Vegetable Gardening Almanac* and is a recognized authority and lecturer on year-round gardening in the Northwest. She is researching and writing a historical novel for young adults, enjoys finding Chinese recipes for winter vegetables, maintains an "indoor jungle," and writes a poem a year for good measure.

GARDENING BOOKS FOR THE PACIFIC NORTHWEST
from Sasquatch Books

Our gardening books are available at bookstores and selected garden centers throughout the Pacifc Northwest. If you wish to order copies by mail, fill out the order form below and return it to us with your payment.

Winter Gardening in the Maritime Northwest
Cool Season Crops for the Year-Round Gardener
by Binda Colebrook

$10.95 × quantity _____ = _____

Growing Vegetables West of the Cascades
Steve Solomon's Complete Guide to Natural Gardening
by Steve Solomon

$14.95 × quantity _____ = _____

The Year in Bloom
Gardening for All Seasons in the Pacific Northwest
by Ann Lovejoy

$11.95 × quantity _____ = _____

Three Years in Bloom
A Garden-Keeper's Journal
by Ann Lovejoy

$14.95 × quantity _____ = _____

Subtotal _____

Washington state residents add 8.1% sales tax . . . . ._____
Postage and handling—add $1.00 per book . . . . ._____

Total order = $ _____

☐ I have enclosed payment of $_____.
   (Please make check or money order payable to Sasquatch Books.)

☐ Please charge this order to my credit card.
   MasterCard #_____ Expiration date_____
   VISA #_____ Expiration date_____
Name_____
Address_____
City_____ State_____ Zip_____

Payment must accompany order.
All orders are sent fourth-class book rate.
Please allow three to six weeks for delivery.

☐ Please send me a free catalog of Sasquatch Book titles.

☐ I would like to use the books as a fundraiser for my club or organization.
   Please send me a discount schedule for bulk orders.

SASQUATCH BOOKS
1931 Second Avenue, Seattle, WA 98101   (206) 441-5555

NOTES

NOTES

NOTES

NOTES

NOTES

NOTES

NOTES

NOTES

NOTES

NOTES